What Do You Do When You Can't Call A Cop?

by Janice A. Seifert
with Billy D. Conley

ULTIMATE SURVIVORS, INC.

CLAREMORE, OKLAHOMA

What Do You Do When You Can't Call A Cop?

Janice A. Seifert

© 1997 by Ultimate Survivors, Inc.

Library of Congress Catalog Card Number: 97-90253

ISBN 0-9657443-0-2

PUBLISHED AND DISTRIBUTED BY:
Ultimate Survivors, Inc.
P. O. Box 2036
Claremore, OK 74018

COVER ART BY JAI SCOTT.

BOOK AND COVER DESIGN BY CARL BRUNE.

PRINTED IN THE UNITED STATES OF AMERICA
BY PARKER PRINTING, INC., TULSA, OKLAHOMA.

JANICE A. SEIFERT

As one of the first female rookie police officers to work a solo graveyard shift patrol on the streets of Tulsa, Oklahoma in 1975, Janice quickly realized that the Police Academy had not adequately prepared her for the physical challenges of the job. The self defense, custody and control tactics she had been taught were unsuitable and inadequate for her 5'2", 110 lb. frame, particularly when a rowdy 250 pounder wanted to resist arrest, or worse. It became a matter of personal survival to develop strategies and techniques to safely incapacitate larger, stronger assailants.

Due to the rapid increase in violent crime over the past two decades, Janice recognized that it wasn't only police officers that needed better, more efficient street survival skills, but the average citizen as well. She found that very few people really know how to protect themselves from a violent attack, nor do they know what makes them a target in the first place. Crime prevention and personal self defense instruction has been her focus since the late 1970s, with programs for men, women, teens, and children. With homicide being the No. 2 cause of death at work, her corporate workplace violence prevention programs have been increasingly in demand.

Public education is a welcome change for this Los Angeles, California native, whose previous experience as a Police Officer included patrol, traffic accident investigation, juvenile crime, and undercover vice, narcotics and prostitution details in both Tulsa, Oklahoma and Dallas, Texas. In addition, she has acted as a bodyguard for numerous dignitaries such as Israel's Defense Minister, Moshe Ahrens, and the Rev. Jesse Jackson.

In late 1991 Janice and a few highly motivated veteran officers decided to become *proactive* instead of *reactive* and created Ultimate Survivors, Inc. As President and Chief Executive Officer of this Oklahoma corporation, Janice, and her specially trained team of off-duty, commissioned law enforcement officers conduct corporate safety and security seminars, teach hands-on self-defense, child safety/anti-abduction programs, perform security inspections of homes and businesses, and provide bodyguards and security officers to private individuals and companies throughout the United States. Janice has an ongoing collaborative relationship with local television and radio stations as a crime prevention expert and has been featured in numerous newspaper articles and industry journals. In 1992 Janice received a U.S. Dept. of Justice "Award for Public Service".

Janice, and her husband, Charlie, a 26 year veteran of the Tulsa Police Department, are the parents of three grown sons, and reside on a wooded acreage northeast of Tulsa with their pet parrots.

BILLY D. CONLEY

*B*ill was born in Clayton, Oklahoma and attended school there and in Los Angeles, California before enlisting in the U.S. Army. After completing his military service, he began his police career in 1962 with the Mesquite, Texas Police Department, attaining the rank of Sergeant in less than four years. In his pursuit of law enforcement challenges, Bill joined the ranks of the Tulsa Police Department in 1967, and served in the Patrol, Traffic Investigation, and Service Divisions. After his retirement in 1987 from Tulsa, his love for police work led him to further serve as a Sergeant in the Criminal Investigation Division and as Jail Director with the Rogers County, Oklahoma Sheriff's Office until hip replacement surgeries forced his retirement as a street officer in March of 1994.

During his law enforcement career Bill was also in charge of security for a chain of fast food restaurants and a Tulsa Bank, and helped develop security programs and institute safety procedures for a number of other retail establishments.

Since retirement, Bill has begun work on a book of short stories, a fiction novel, and has published several poems which earned him a nomination for membership into the International Society of Poets. Bill is also currently involved in extensive criminal research relating to major unsolved crimes. He and his wife, Janet, reside in Northeastern Oklahoma.

★ TABLE OF CONTENTS ★

*This is dedicated to our respective spouses,
Charlie Seifert and Janet Conley,
without whose love, encouragement,
constructive criticism and endless patience,
this book would not have been written.*

★ ACKNOWLEDGMENTS ★

*N*o one becomes a self-defense expert without many years of actual street fighting experience and extensive training and input from many instructors, mentors and associates throughout the years. These many valuable contributions have allowed the authors to assemble and develop their own unique version of "field tested" theories and techniques. Useful bits of information and new strategies are constantly filtering in from countless sources around the world, wherever a story surfaces about a surviving victim who outmaneuvered his or her attacker. Since "street survival" for citizens is a relatively new concept, it is not a rigid discipline with strict rules of conduct or procedure. As crime changes and evolves, so do self defense and crime prevention methods.

Among the many valuable contributors in the field of personal self defense, special thanks is due to the members of the American Women's Self Defense Association (AWSDA) for their continuing support of education and training programs designed to protect women and children from the criminal element in our society, with special gratitude to Elizabeth Kennedy, President. Phil Messina, retired N.Y.P.D. homicide detective and current President and Instructor of Modern Warrior in New York has been an additional source of inspiration for the past five years.

Additionally, we wish to express sincere gratitude to all the Police Officers, Liaison Officers and Interpreters of the Metropolitan Police Department of Tokyo, Japan, as well as officers with the Imperial Police (Palace Guard), who graciously assisted us and provided invaluable information and street survival tips during a visit to their city. Special thanks to Akiyoshi Kauchi, Masataka Ishizuka and Yoshiko Yanase for spending so much of their valuable time with us.

The author's appreciation extends to the following specially trained and very dedicated police officers who donate their off-duty time as staff instructors for Ultimate Survivors, Inc., to teach citizens how to protect themselves, and some of whom graciously donated additional time to pose for the demonstrative illustrations in this manuscript. These officers are: Sr. Patrolman C. A. Seifert, Jr., Mike Parsons, Danielle Bishop, Master Patrolman Steve Bass, Mathias Wicks, Michael Avey, Danny Siebert, and Rodney Russo, all Tulsa, Oklahoma Police Officers; and Sgt. Wayne Stinnett of the Claremore, Oklahoma Police Department. Additional research information not readily available in the "stacks" of published or public data we combed was provided by Bill Cook, a homicide investigator with the Oklahoma City Police Department; George Sunderland, Manager of Criminal Justice Services for the American Association of Retired Persons (AARP); Guy Toscano at the Bureau of Labor Statistics, U.S. Department of Labor, Washington, D.C; and Richard Cosier of the University of Oklahoma.

We also wish to thank juvenile models Amber and Mitchell Conley, and senior models Raymond and Ginny McCarty along with Margaret Andrew for their participation in this project. The photographs which form a very vital part of this manuscript could not have been possible without the help of two free-lance photographers, Donald Bordwine and Mike McNally who generously donated their time on numerous occasions.

We want to offer a special thanks to April Nowland, Trades and Technical Acquistions Editor for the McGraw-Hill Inc. Professional Book Group. Her belief in our project kept us going and pushing to find a motivated agent and publisher.

Finally, we must recognize the woman who first realized that we must write this book and offer it to all citizens, and insisted that we had the talent and knowledge to do so, and who continued to "nag" us until it was completed. That special lady is Kathy Wanenmacher whose life, like that of many of us, has been touched by the criminal element in our society.

What Do You Do When You Can't Call A Cop?

After taking their money and valuables, the armed robbers force a restaurant manager, his employees and remaining customers into the cooler at the rear of the building. The victims are *told* this is to allow the perpetrators time to escape before police can be called. Once inside the limited, isolated space of the cooler, however, all of the victims are executed with shots to the head.

At a nearby mall, a few department store customers look on casually as a man leads a tearful little girl outside. When she resists and protests noisily as he places her in his vehicle, their sympathies are for the "father" who has to put up with such a brat. A few days later, hikers will find her horribly abused body, discarded in a wooded area just outside of town. The man is not family.

In another city, an apartment complex parking lot is dark and secluded. As a woman resident who routinely parks there approaches her car, she is attacked. She tries to ward off her assailant, but in less than a minute she is out-muscled and over-whelmed, unable to escape the punishment. She will be found, dazed and wandering, by a passerby. She has been beaten, raped and is suffering from multiple injuries, both physical and psycho-logical. In addition, unknown to her as yet, she has been exposed to the deadly AIDS virus.

Elsewhere, a man decides to resist the knife wielding youth who demands the cash he has just withdrawn from the automatic teller. In less than three minutes the man will be dead from a single "defense" wound to the inside of his forearm. He leaves behind a wife and three young children.

While the elderly man and his wife attend their church services on Sunday, burglars remove everything of value from their modest home, then set fire to the dwelling, destroying a lifetime of posses-sions and memories.

The preceding scenarios are not excerpts from a novel, or scenes from a movie. They are descriptions of real incidents — stories that have repeatedly made headlines in your daily newspaper and been lead stories on your local television and radio news. Of the *43.6 million criminal victimizations* that were described in the most recent annual National Crime Victimization Survey, 10.9 million were rapes, robberies, or assaults. There were nearly 25,000 murders. Among the almost 100 million households in the United States, there were more than *32 million property crimes.*

The robbery and murder of restaurant employees and customers has occurred many times in this country during recent years. For example, in July of 1978 in Oklahoma City, Oklahoma, six people at a Sirloin Stockade Restaurant were killed by a gunman who had only hours before murdered a family of three. A McDonalds Restaurant in San Ysidro, California in early 1984 was the scene of a bloodbath perpetrated by a single gunman. Armed with an automatic rifle, his siege of terror lasted 82 minutes during which 22 people were killed and 43 wounded. It finally ended with a bullet from a police sharpshooter. In August of 1992, during a robbery at a Lee's Chicken Restaurant in Tulsa, Oklahoma, four young employees were marched into a back room and forced to kneel for their subsequent executions. These are only a few of the literally thousands of such cases nationwide.

Over the past several years, we have been bombarded with news stories and images of workplace violence. We have heard about postal employees going berserk; fast food restaurant employees and customers alike gunned down; shoppers sprayed with bullets; a man who killed eight people at a San Francisco law firm which he blamed for his business failures; convenience store clerks shot for the few dollars in the till. Nationwide, more than 26 people are murdered in their workplace *each week.*

Could the victims have done anything that might have changed the outcome of those tragedies? Probably! Unfortunately, they did not recognize the warning signs indicating what was to come, which were evident at the outset of these incidents. We will be discussing those "red flags" and how early detection can increase survival odds for victims of workplace violence.

In the past, most corporate safety and security policies, if present at all, have dealt primarily with loss prevention and ways to protect the *business*. Since the infamous bombing of the Federal Building in Oklahoma City which killed 168 people and injured more than 400 on April 19, 1995, concern about workplace violence has increased and some proactive employers have attempted to take steps to reduce the risk of violent episodes at work. Suggestions will be made here on how to reduce the probability of such acts by specific written policies and procedures, employee training, and strategic security hardware and personnel. However, no matter how good security is, random acts of violence are impossible to predict. It behooves each individual to learn the techniques, understand the risks, and formulate their own self defense plan.

Outside the workplace, every parent in this country has probably been made painfully aware of stories about the terrible crimes committed against our children. Adam Walsh and Polly Klaus are names that frequently surface as sad reminders of promising young lives snuffed out by child molesters and kidnappers. But one of the horrifying things about these crimes against children is that they are not always perpetrated by adults. One such case was a small boy in England who became separated from his mother and was taken from a store by two boys only a few years older than he was. Even though many people later recalled seeing him being pulled along by these boys, no one intervened. He was later found mutilated and murdered. Another instance in West Memphis, Arkansas, involved the murder of young boys riding their bicycles. They were also victims of a young predator. The number of stranger abductions, molestations and murders, however, are only a fraction of the child victimizations that are perpetrated by *known* acquaintances!

There are many things we can teach our children that will increase their chances of survival and reduce the likelihood of abduction. It is not necessary for them to emulate cartoon superheros or become martial arts students in order to thwart abduction or molestation attempts, but it is necessary that they know how to recognize a dangerous situation and how to deal with it. We will provide guidelines for children and parents to help them make these determinations and reduce risks. We will also suggest several effective physical resistance techniques.

Violence against women is a problem that is increasingly being acknowledged in our nation. Studies and annual crime reports show that rape and spousal abuse is increasing even as certain other major crimes show decline. Robbery and assaults are increasing for our older women. A recent national survey conducted by the National Victim Center in Arlington, Virginia, and a survey conducted in Tulsa, Oklahoma in 1993, suggest that *one out of every two women in America will be sexually abused or raped* at least once during her life.

Most experts agree that at least 8 in 10 women do not report the crime of rape, for a variety of reasons which we will discuss in a later chapter. In 1993 an Oklahoma research report called "Rape, Tulsa Women Speak Out", was prepared by the Tulsa Institute of Behavioral Sciences in collaboration with the Tulsa Police Department, the Tulsa Sexual Assault Nurse Examiners Program, the District Attorney's office, and the Tulsa Psychiatric Center. This study estimated the actual number of women raped in Tulsa each year at approximately *2,500*, compared to approximately 250–300 rapes actually reported during the same time period. This ratio is typical and is repeated in cities throughout the U.S. Unfortunately, because of the low numbers of rapes reported, the magnitude of the problem goes unrecognized by the general public and, in some cases, even law enforcement agencies.

The violence faced by older women should not be overlooked. The Mother's Day Report, released by the Older Women's League in 1994 contains some eye-opening figures: 400,000 older women, living in institutions, are victims of physical or sexual abuse each year; A 30% increase in the murder rate for women 65 years or older from 1974 to 1990; Women over 65 were mugged at or near their homes twice as often as younger women, and 75% of those assaults occurred during the daytime; 1 in 100 women between the ages of 50 and 64 becomes a victim of violent crime each year. This book will give practical information on how to recognize, prevent and survive such attacks and outline common con games directed at senior citizens.

No one who uses an automatic teller machine (ATM) expects to die from a knife wound, or from any violent attack, after making a withdrawal. It happens. Knife wounds are nasty, and death can be almost instantaneous. Six lethal targets on the body can produce death in less than two minutes. Common "defense wounds" can result in unconsciousness and death in as little as *14 seconds*. Would you know how to react to increase your odds of survival in the event of a knife attack? Hopefully you will have the information necessary to formulate a successful defense plan after reading the following chapters.

Unfortunately, when writing a book of this nature, it is necessary to concentrate on, and draw attention to, worst case scenarios such as knife attacks, murders and rapes. We must also target unsavory segments of our society, for example our teenage offenders. While this group constitutes only about 7% of all teens, they commit a disproportionately high number of violent offenses. Most teenagers take an interest in our society, abide by the rules, and do many things to help their communities. We must, however, acknowledge the significant danger from gangs and youthful criminals, many of whom began their criminal career as early as 8 or 10 years of age. The trend is clear and significant. More violent crimes are committed by this group per capita than any other and the percentage is rising. Based on birth records, this age group is expected to increase nearly 25% during the next decade. We believe we have seen only the tip of the iceberg, with law enforcement, and the justice and corrections system, unprepared and unable to deal effectively with this problem.

The fact that our streets are dangerous must be acknowledged. You cannot prepare for what you don't expect to happen, and you must recognize that bad things don't just happen to *other* people. Without that acknowledgment you will not take proper precautionary measures nor memorize methods of self-defense for you or your loved ones. We <u>can</u> defend ourselves, legally and effectively. It is hoped that this book will offer practical and beneficial suggestions that will increase your personal safety and security. Naturally, we advise that you check your state and local laws with regard to the legal use of deadly force and self-defense actions, as well as any weaponry you may consider using. Many state statutes differ on what is, and is *not,* legal.

If you read this book and follow the advice found on its pages, do we guarantee that you will not be a crime victim or be injured in a violent incident? No! Only the Supreme Being can make that guarantee. Are we going to make you experts in the Martial Arts? No! Those skills need to be taught in person, hands-on, by an expert. You cannot learn them from reading a book. You can, however, learn the following: how to improve your survival instincts; understand crime trends and offenders; improve your security precautions at home and at work; learn to recognize signals that can help you decide when to take self-protective actions; what works and what doesn't in terms of weaponry currently on the market; when and how to best disable an assailant in the least amount of time, with minimum risk to you; and how to better protect your children. Employers can learn ways to improve worker and customer safety and limit civil liability.

Remember, the average criminal looks for an <u>easy</u> target. The authors believe the information contained herein will, if implemented, make you a <u>harder</u> target, one not favored by criminals, and one prepared to <u>survive</u> a violent confrontation. We want you all to have a better chance of making it to the next family gathering.

JANICE A. SEIFERT
BILLY D. CONLEY

CHAPTER ONE

PREVENTION AND PREPARATION

Practical Crime Prevention Measures

*I*t is always preferable to avoid a fight rather than to have one. There are many effective ways to reduce the likelihood that you will be selected as a crime victim. There are two types of crime victims — random and specific. While there is no way to guarantee you that you will never be a crime victim, it is much easier to avoid random victimizations than it is to avoid someone who specifically wants <u>you</u> or <u>your property</u>. If someone has targeted you or wants inside your home badly enough, they can probably get to you in spite of your precautions. It is likely you will have a personal confrontation with this individual sooner or later. Most victimizations, however, *can* be avoided.

Certain safeguards can be put in place in and around your residence. Home security systems are helpful to warn you of an intrusion if you are home and can warn neighbors and notify police. An audible alarm may discourage the "garden variety" burglar, but any alarm system can be defeated. Remember, the system is only as good as the person installing it. Be sure to pick a reputable company. Check around and ask for references. What is the location of the monitoring operator? If you live in Kansas City and the alarm is monitored in Dallas you can imagine the problems and time involved in relaying the intrusion alarm information to your local police or sheriff's department, not to mention the difficulty if directions are needed to locate your home. Be sure it is monitored locally. Find out whether it "captures" your phone line when it is activated, preventing you from calling anyone for help. Find out whether it can be deactivated from the outside of your home by cutting your phone lines, or if you can get the kind that automatically sends a "panic alarm" to the monitoring company if a phone interruption occurs. Find out what happens to your alarm if there is a power outage (often a time when thieves become very active). Bottom line, know what you are buying. Know the limitations of your system. Portable, single door and personal alarms also are available and may have some effect against the casual intruder.

Dogs are usually good "alarms" to alert you to anyone approaching your home, and have a deterrent effect on most casual burglars. No burglar wants the noise they make or the likelihood of being bitten. However, if you or your home has been targeted specifically, they know you have a dog, and will take measures to prepare for and eliminate the risk it poses.

If you live in rental housing, tell your landlord if security improvements are needed such as better lighting, stronger locks, peep hole in front door, or night security guards. All are ways to make a building safer. Always lock your doors and windows. Insist on a new lock when you move into an apartment or other rental. Find out who else has a key and how accessible it is to others, such as office or maintenance personnel and even the general public. Spring for a good 2 inch deadbolt, rather than a chainlock, but realize that if it doesn't bolt into a solid frame or stud, the whole door, frame and all, can be kicked in.

Secure your home as well as possible and form a plan for escape or defense if the security is breached. Keep your garage door locked. It can provide easy access to your home, and also offer a variety of tools to assist a burglar who wishes to break into your house. These tools can become dangerous weapons once he is inside. All he has to do is close the garage door behind him and he has complete privacy to do as he wishes. Do not hide a key outside — anywhere! Any place you can think of to hide a key, they can think of to look. The average burglar commits up to 118 burglaries a year. He gets good at it.

Keep all your entrances well-lit, and keep curtains or blinds tightly closed at night or when privacy dictates. Go outside your home or apartment at night, after you have shut your window coverings, and determine what can still be seen by someone attempting to peek in your windows. You may be astonished at what can be clearly seen by someone determined to look in. Take advantage of timers both inside and out to turn lamps and radios on and off automatically, so that it looks and sounds as though people (plural) are home. Motion-sensitive lighting is relatively inexpensive.

Make sure outside bushes and shrubbery are trimmed. Be aware of potential hiding places and avoid them. Poorly lit parking areas and walkways are always hazardous.

If strangers come to your door and ask to use your phone in an emergency, offer to make the call yourself. Ask them to wait *outside* while you make the call for them. Offer to call the police for them. Any *legitimate* person in distress would welcome the police. Even if they indicate they don't want you to call 911, do it anyway for your own protection. Don't be fooled by a woman or a young person — they could be decoys and their accomplice could be hiding in the bushes or outside your field of vision until the decoy gains entrance. It could be a set-up to a robbery situation. Never give strangers information about who is or is not at home or personal information about your neighbors and their habits, even if the party claims to be a long-lost relative or a close friend.

Determine the identity of a visitor before opening your door. Beware of people you are not expecting, even if they claim to be police officers or utility personnel. Anyone can buy a uniform and a badge. (Would you know a *real* badge from a fake? Even officers from neighboring cities have different types of badges — there are hundreds, possibly thousands, of different kinds). Check sales and service representatives by calling their companies. *Real* police officers have a commission card signed by their police chief and sheriff's deputies have one signed by their Sheriff. They must show it to you if you ask to see it for I.D. verification. Verify with police headquarters (call 911) or utility company management the assignment at your address if you did not call them. In rental housing, never take the word of an unexpected maintenance person that they need in your apartment without checking with management. If it is at night and the office is closed, call security or tell them to come back another time. Verify with the local utility company if a service representative or maintenance person tells you there is a gas or electric emergency in your unit that will require them to gain entrance.

Keep emergency phone numbers handy by each phone. You will have no time to hunt for them or look them up if you really need them. Know your neighbors. Be aware of those you can trust in an emergency.

If you come home and find a door or window open or signs of forced entry, *don't go in!* Go to the nearest safe phone and call the police. If you rush in to see what happened, you not only destroy evidence, but run a distinct risk of coming upon the burglars and facing a violent confrontation.

A general rule of thumb about burglars. The vast majority of them would prefer to target dwellings that they believe to be unoccupied. They do not want to be seen and they don't want any trouble. They want to get in, get what they want, and get out with the least possible risk. They don't want to confront you and are not as likely to have a weapon (unless they find one in your house). Obviously, then, it would make sense to keep your home looking and sounding occupied at all times (preferably by two or more people). Again inexpensive automatic timers are a possible answer. Be advised, however, the intruder who deliberately breaks into a dwelling that he knows or believes to be occupied is truly one of the most dangerous criminals out there. He is obviously prepared for a face-to-face confrontation and undoubtedly has an agenda beyond just a simple burglary. He is likely to be armed with one or more weapons and has planned to commit a robbery, rape, aggravated assault or even murder. You must know in advance what you are able and *willing* to do in such a situation. For example, if you have decided that you would probably shoot such an intruder, would the sudden realization that he is probably only 12 or 13 years old prevent you from doing so? Is a young perpetrator any less likely to injure or kill you? The experts say no, and point out that the young criminals have less to fear from the justice system even if they are caught and convicted. Many states now find that nearly half of all burglars arrested are juveniles, with thousands under the age of 10.

Avoiding victimization also requires taking personal safety precautions outside your home, whether you are at work, shopping, or enjoying a recreational activity. The odds of becoming a victim in the workplace will be discussed in a later chapter.

Always try to stay in well-lighted areas. Be alert and walk confidently, directly to your destination at a steady pace, paying close attention to what is going on around you.

The "bad guys" don't jump up out of the sidewalk cracks. They cannot complete a "surprise attack" if you see them coming. They are much less likely to pursue an individual who is making eye contact with them than someone who apparently doesn't notice them. You appear to be a much more aggressive person if you make eye contact. Additionally, if they *do* attempt to confront or follow you, you can better prepare for a counterattack both physically and mentally if you are aware of the situation up front.

Walk or jog on the side of the street facing traffic, so that no vehicle can creep up behind you. Walk close to the curb. Avoid doorways, bushes and alleys where attackers can hide.

It is especially important to vary your routine. Don't always take the same route, park in the same spot, leave at the same time, or jog on the same path. An attacker will usually "case" or stalk his victim and learn their habits. He may then carefully select the appropriate location for his attack, knowing when you will pass that spot. If you have a very set schedule, it also makes it very easy for a burglar to know when he can enter your home. The more unpredictable you are, the more difficult a target you become.

Wear clothes and shoes that give you freedom of movement. Don't burden yourself with packages or a purse. (How can you be the victim of a purse snatching if you are not carrying a purse?) You cannot possibly *need* everything you normally carry in a large purse. You are just carrying a present for someone who doesn't want to work for a living. Consider a "fanny-pack" if you must carry more than will fit into your pockets. However, a fanny- pack probably takes you out of the realm of purse snatchings and places you at risk from a robbery because you have sorted all the "trash" from your purse and are now only carrying the "good stuff" which can't be "snatched" because it is strapped to your waist. Therefore, a perpetrator will have to make you give it to him, by force or fear. Major credit cards (only one at a time, please), cash and identification should be carried in a front pants pocket (to avoid pickpockets). Parcels or briefcases also increase your likelihood of victimization and tend to distract you from your objective — getting to your vehicle or home safely. Using "Parcel Pickup" at department stores is a good, safe way to load your numerous purchases.

Be careful when people stop you for directions. Always reply from a safe distance and never get too close to someone in a car. You do not have to be a "human map" or a good Samaritan when you are alone and vulnerable. That's what the police are for. If you want to help someone who appears to be stranded or in trouble, go to a safe phone and call 911.

If you believe you are being followed, go to a well-lighted, crowded, public area or to a police or fire station or substation (they are open all night). <u>Do not go home!</u> Don't lead them to your home. Honk your horn to attract attention. There have been numerous instances where intended victims turned *drive-<u>thru's</u>* into *drive-<u>ins</u>* in successful efforts to avoid victimization. Insurance is a wonderful thing! Even if insurance doesn't happen to cover the property damage you may cause, such as the cost of a window, for example, it is cheap compared to the value of a human life. If you feel you are in danger, don't be reluctant to yell, run or fight back. If you are in trouble, attract help any way you can. Yell loudly, break a window in an occupied house, activate a personal alarm, etc.

When parking, stay near lighted areas. Check anything or anyone that appears suspicious before leaving your car. If complete safety is questionable, park or even shop elsewhere.

Always lock your car, but don't assume that because you locked it when you left it, no one could have breached that security and hidden inside. It only takes a few seconds for someone to defeat most lock mechanisms. If it is <u>you</u> they want, they can relock the door and then hide inside. Check the back seat and floorboards before you open the door to your vehicle. Then, in the following order: 1) get in quickly; 2) lock the doors immediately; 3) start the engine; 4) then, with the Park gear on, fasten seatbelts and secure any children or infants in their seats after you are locked inside your car.

If your car breaks down on a major road or highway, activate flashers, stay inside and wait for help. This would be a great time for a car phone (preferably one with its own battery source, in case your car battery is dead). Remember, however, that cellular phones are easily monitored, and be cautious what you say to whoever you call to help you. Highway Patrol can be reached by dialing *55 in most states. Check that number in your state if you are a frequent traveler. Whether or not you have a car phone, keep an index card with a quarter taped to it with emergency phone numbers to give to someone who might offer assistance. Roll down your car window just enough to stick the card through. If your rescuer is really a good Samaritan, they will make the calls for you and get you help. If not, you only lost a quarter, you didn't risk your life.

Establish a buddy system when leaving your workplace. After hours, let building security know if you are working alone. Avoid elevators with suspicious strangers. Wait for the next car. If you must ride, stand close to the control panel. Avoid stairwells, public restrooms, ATM machines, deserted laundry rooms and/or parking garages. If possible, lock your office door when alone.

Never forget that there is one thing that every criminal needs in order to commit his crime — *uninterrupted privacy!* If he feels confident that he will not be disturbed, seen, or heard, then he has ideal conditions for his deviant behavior. That is why it is so vital that you guard against providing potential criminals with this circumstance. For example, in a kidnapping or abduction attempt, the perpetrator(s) need to separate the victim from populated areas and take them to a hiding place. They cannot commit the balance of their crime, such as rape, robbery, murder, or request for ransom, in a public place where others can see and hear what is going on. Every effort must be made to resist such an abduction, since the situation will not improve thereafter, but will worsen significantly. Even if a weapon is present, perhaps especially if a weapon is present, your safety may hinge on whether anyone else can see or hear what is going on. Few criminals are willing to risk using a firearm, for example, in a very public place where it will draw attention to them, and what they are attempting to do. However, once they have you alone, and are finished with you, they are likely to use it to keep you from testifying against them. Are there any guarantees you will survive an abduction attempt if you resist? No, however the odds are strongly in your favor if you do, and very much against you if you don't. Every situation is different, and you must use your common sense to determine appropriate action. More information to help you make this decision will follow in later chapters.

In general, be alert to your surroundings and make every effort to avoid being involved in a dangerous situation. Take the time to practice common sense safety measures and apply them to your daily routine. Channel your energy to work for you to reduce your fear and minimize the chance of being victimized.

Survival Instincts

*E*very living organism has an instinct to survive. Unfortunately, humans seem to be the only species that actually attempt to suppress it. The more "civilized" we become, the more we resist and ignore the facts and warning signs that tell us we are in danger. It is not *fashionable* to admit fear or concern for ones safety. You may feel you risk being a social outcast or being labeled a weakling if you show fear openly, or chance being called a "rambo type" if you actively discuss safety precautions or take security measures due to a perceived or actual danger to you, your family or your possessions.

Now let's discuss the four-letter "F" word —FEAR! What *is* fear? We've all heard the phrase "frozen with fear," or "I was too frightened to move." We've read accounts of victims who stated "I was so scared I couldn't even scream." Can fear incapacitate us? *Not* if we realize that fear is just a four-letter word meaning "adrenalin with nowhere to go." Every time something out-of-the-ordinary happens and you are startled by something, your body has an automatic emergency alarm system. Every animal has this "startle reflex." Your heart starts to beat faster, your mouth may become dry, you may start to sweat, have goosebumps, get a strange feeling in the back of your throat or "butterflies" in your stomach. This is all caused by a sudden burst of adrenalin, a powerful, naturally produced drug. Simply put, when your heart is beating faster you can burn more calories than you normally would. This means you can fight harder, be stronger, run faster, get madder and so forth.

The stories of young mothers of slender build lifting vehicles off their trapped children are true. Fantastic tales abound of unusual strength, bravery and incredible survival of not only police officers and firemen, but of ordinary citizens who are quickly called heros or examples of "superhuman power and endurance." They all have at least one thing in common. They effectively used that chemical "charge" to allow them to perform tasks that they normally would not have been able to do. Conversely, individuals who do not recognize the physical advantage that this adrenalin boost produces, or are unable or unwilling to utilize it, often begin to shake, to find they can only speak in a whisper, to sweat profusely and may find movement awkward (remember when you had to give that unexpected oral report in school and were unprepared, or had your first on-stage speaking role in a play?). Remember, this is a powerful stimulant and if not used and burned up may have some temporary side effects. Knowing and expecting this phenomenon to occur upon the sudden realization that a violent confrontation may be imminent, and realizing that it is a natural part of the survival instinct designed for your express benefit, will allow you to use it effectively and resist the urge to call it "the f-word". Let it energize you, not paralyze you.

Men are "expected" to know naturally how to protect themselves and their families and frequently have difficulty admitting that they really have no actual knowledge of how to fight effectively, having had little or no actual training in street survival or hand-to-hand combat. Martial arts training, while a valuable learning experience, and one that improves ones mind and body, requires a substantial time commitment, is not for everyone, and is, in general, ineffective and unsuitable against most violent criminal assaults, multiple attacker situations and armed attacks. *There are no rules in a street fight, and it cannot be choreographed in advance. A gang will not jump you one at a time — there is no honorable fight in the street.* Most individuals who have had military combat training, have never actually used it, don't practice or think about it frequently, and therefore have forgotten the bulk of it, limited as it was. Even contact sports such as wrestling or boxing are no guarantee of protection against violence. Granted, some principles from all of these activities are useful, but you need *more.* You need quicker, easier, more efficient tactics. A street fight is not a sanctioned, supervised "match" between individuals of equal skill, size and strength. Criminals rarely instigate a *fair* fight and are usually better prepared, superior to their victims in size and strength, and possibly armed with a weapon. It is a struggle for survival; life or death.

While it is not "macho" to be *paranoid*, it is essential to be *prepared*. Preparedness is a trait that is much valued. However, one cannot prepare for that which he does not expect to happen, or does not understand. If your loved ones depend on you for their safety, you may all be in trouble. If you can't save yourself, how can you help them? It is vital that every member of the family learn what they can do to protect themselves and reduce the likelihood that they will be the victim of a criminal attack. Men's confrontational situations are usually different from those of women and young children, but are more likely to involve a weapon or great bodily force. With the growing numbers of youth gangs throughout the country, multiple attacker situations and carjackings are more frequent than ever before, and males are usually the targets.

Women in our society are raised as nurturers and caretakers. They are taught to respond to and treat injuries, not cause them. In spite of the increasing numbers of women in what were traditionally men's occupations, society still strongly suggests that women must be gentle, sympathetic, "girlish" or "motherly", and above all look *feminine*. This usually means tight, restrictive, often revealing clothing, and fragile, wobbly footwear, totally unsuited to strenuous physical activities such as running, kicking or fighting. Women are taught when they are young to rely on their fathers or brothers, and later on look to boyfriends, husbands, sons or other male acquaintances for physical protection. They grow up expecting to be "rescued" if they are in danger. How often have women been told to "scream for help", if they are assaulted, or "call the police" if they sense danger. They are advised to "run away" from an attacker.

Women are not usually told that screams for help are often ignored because people either don't want to get involved or, as police are often told after an attack, the screams sounded like children playing. They aren't told that even the fastest female (in <u>good</u> running shoes) cannot run as fast as the fastest male. And after he catches up to her, she has to fight him, and she is out of breath from the chase. Additionally they are not informed that most women who experience a violent confrontation are injured or killed long before help arrives. They are not told that the average response time for a priority one police emergency call is 7 to 10 minutes, the average fight is 3 minutes long, and the average female can only respond with full physical efficiency for 30–45 seconds before she begins to run out of breath, strength and loses the potential tactical advantage of surprise (when she returns the attack rather than retreating or submitting). Females are repeatedly told that they are physically incapable of successfully fighting a larger, stronger attacker. They are programmed to believe that if they have such a confrontation they will lose — so they don't even try. They don't plan a counter-attack because they don't believe it will be successful.

Size has little to do with how effective a fighter can be. Consider small creatures, weighing only a few pounds, such as cats, squirrels, rabbits, etc. A 300 lb. person that picks one up when it doesn't wish to be touched will sustain substantial injuries — certainly serious enough to release the creature. Even though they are small, they use their natural weapons effectively. Have you ever been playing with your small child and suddenly been nearly "cold cocked" when their head strikes you under the chin, or temporarily blinded when their fingers poke your eyes. A small child can effectively knock the wind out of a much larger person by simply head-butting them in the stomach.

Again, size is not a significant factor in determining who will win a fight. The various natural "weapons" that we all possess will be discussed in the coming pages.

You cannot solve a problem by refusing to admit it exists. As an American citizen the odds of becoming a victim of violent crime have increased more than 500% since the 1960's according to a Washington D.C. "think tank" organization called "Safe Streets Alliance". America is the *most violent* civilized country in the world. Nearly 11 million violent victimizations are reported each year in the U.S. and the F.B.I. has estimated that only 38% of all violent crimes are actually reported. Two different surveys, one in 1989 by the Bureau of Justice Statistics, and another by a major metropolitan police department in 1991 agreed that approximately 1 out of every 46 adults nationwide is currently under the care or custody of a corrections agency (approximately 4.1 million adults). At least a million of them are *not* incarcerated, and are currently out on parole, probation, or bond, awaiting trial. These numbers just reflect the criminals we know about who have already entered the system. What about all the perpetrators of the crimes that weren't reported? A Rand Corporation study of prison inmates found that the average inmate had committed 187 crimes the year before being incarcerated.

Many small, rural communities are now, surprisingly, experiencing a higher per capita crime rate than large, admittedly dangerous, metropolitan areas. This is possibly due in part to the fact that there are fewer law enforcement officers in small towns, people feel safer, are less suspicious, and less likely to initiate security precautions. This makes them easy targets. If there is one thing that criminals want, its an easy target. The more difficult the crime is to pull off, or the more difficult it *appears*, the less likely it is to happen. How else could they commit an average of 187 crimes per year?

Failure to accept the fact that you are at risk from violent criminal acts each and every day of your life, for whatever reason, is unrealistic and means that you will probably take no precautions to avoid or prevent victimization. Realization and acceptance of the everpresent dangers of our society allows you to become aware of your survival instincts, enhance, enrich and hone them to sharpness, rather than ignore and deny them by choosing to believe either "It won't happen to me", or "I can't do anything about it".

Do not expect to be "rescued". ***You are responsible for your own personal safety.*** The chances are great that no one else will be present when you are victimized and every second counts. Use those moments efficiently. Don't waste valuable time looking for help. That doesn't mean you should not call 911 if you are able and have time to do so before the assailant reaches you. However, it only takes two or three seconds to kick in most doors and another second or two before the attacker reaches you. Do not rely on help that will not reach you in time.

Once you have accepted the fact that you are a potential target, and you have a better understanding of your natural survival instincts, you may decide to learn to defend yourself. It may now occur to you that you must consider the consequences of any actions you may take. What if you injure or kill your attacker? There is a distinct possibility that you will cause serious bodily injuries defending yourself effectively. While it is your responsibility to know the statutes regarding the use of deadly force in your state, and to realize they are somewhat different in all states, particularly with regard to weaponry and self-defense equipment, a general rule can be followed in all states. You have an ***absolute right to survive.*** If you *reasonably* believe that your life or that of another (such as your child) is in imminent or immediate danger, you have the right to use deadly force. Deadly force can be used in most states to defend yourself against murder, manslaughter, forcible rape (any rape but statutory rape), forcible sodomy and robbery. However, it must be <u>legal</u> deadly force. For example, in your state a handgun might be legal for personal defense <u>inside</u> your home, however it might be illegal if used <u>outside</u> your home against an assailant. Penal law in most states allows a citizen to counterattack using the same degree, or level, of <u>force</u> that is being used against them, until such time as they can knowingly escape in complete safety (this should not be construed to mean a victim can use the same type of illegal <u>weapon</u>).

Our purposes here, however, are not to discuss or interpret state laws on deadly force, but rather to point out that if you are in the legal defense of your home or your person you need not worry about the welfare of the perpetrator. Again, please make yourself familiar with the laws governing your own state. As for civil liability, remember anyone can sue anyone for nearly anything, but that doesn't mean they will win, and it is a mute point if you didn't survive the confrontation.

Your concern must be for yourself and your family. If you allow something to happen to you, none of them will ever be the same. Your survival is essential to everyone who needs and loves you. Whatever is done to you is done to them. Think of it as a necessary act to protect your loved ones, as well as yourself, if you have any problem with inflicting pain/disability/injury/ death on an attacker. A discussion in a later chapter will elaborate on the likelihood that they are a repeat offender and unable/unwilling to be rehabilitated.

Most states agree that if you are attacked, you have the legal right to continue your counterattack until you believe you can *safely retreat.* Many victims who had successfully "grounded" or wounded their assailant, then tried to run for safety too soon, wrongly assuming that they would not be pursued again. Sadly, when their attacker recaptured them, they were out of breath and couldn't win a second match. If you cannot reach help or safety immediately, do not stop your counter-assault until you are certain you can do so safely. That does not necessarily mean that your assailant must be dead or unconscious. They must, however, be disabled in such a manner that they cannot continue to harm you. We will discuss how you can accomplish this shortly.

Once you begin to fight **do not stop until you have won.** Do not stop because you get hurt. If you fight, you probably will receive some injuries. That is the nature of a fight. However, cuts, bruises, broken bones, missing teeth can all heal or be fixed. Death cannot be fixed. If you contract AIDS from a rape you cannot be cured. If you stop fighting you may very well die. Make up your mind that you <u>will</u> survive. Unfortunately many people facing their first violent confrontation are so psychologically crushed by the knowledge that they have just received a potentially disfiguring or disabling injury that they quit the fight and give up. Usually a perpetrator who will use deadly force or maiming to accomplish his crime will also kill. You <u>can</u> continue to fight effectively with injuries. The vast majority of bullet wounds are not life threatening. *<u>You are probably not going to receive any help for your injuries until you</u>* **<u>disable your attacker.</u>**

Let's dispel one more myth before we go any further. For years we have heard the theory that "if you fight back, you will make your attacker angry and you will be hurt worse". Statistically, that is not likely to be the case. In a government study of more than 4,300,00 violent victimizations, nearly 72% of the victims took some type of self-protective measure to protect themselves. More than 70% of those who took action felt that what they did helped, and did not hurt, the situation. Only 7.3% felt their actions made the situation worse. Are there times when you should comply and not fight? Yes, definitely. A general rule of thumb: If it is your property they want, give it to them, especially if they are armed. If it is <u>you</u> they want, fight. We will be listing factors (red flag situations) that can help you decide whether to take self-protective actions or not as we proceed.

★ CHAPTER TWO ★

CONVENTIONAL WEAPONS — PROS & CONS

Once most people acknowledge that "it is a jungle out there", their first instinct is to acquire some sort of weapon designed to either "blow them away" or "spray them with a magic potion" to make the bad guys disappear. Most people prefer a device that is simple to use, can be used from a distance, does not require contact with the criminal, and can be readily acquired. We want an <u>easy</u>, <u>sanitary</u> method of self-defense. Just as we look for simple, *industrial strength* cleaners to reduce the need for "elbow grease", we seek quick, "no-brainer" methods to eliminate threats to our personal safety, such as guns, sprays, stun guns, whistles and alarms, and countless other innovative creations, which make millions every year for manufacturers and retailers who capitalize on society's fears. Unfortunately, effective self-defense is not that easy.

It is very important to remember that just because an item is available for sale does not guarantee its effectiveness nor its legality. In many jurisdictions it is legal to sell items that cannot legally be used on the streets, and which may not be legal even in your homes. It is *imperative* that you check your local ordinances and statutes regarding the use of self defense items and the *legal use of deadly force*. Further, do not rely on manufacturer's or retailers claims for effectiveness. The Federal Trade Commission (FTC) is constantly on the lookout for misrepresentations and unsubstantiated claims of effectiveness of self-protective equipment. Unfortunately, the public rarely hears about retractions of false advertising claims or penalties levied against the offending companies. The mislead public continues to purchase such items with a false sense of security. Understand the limitations of anything you carry or use for your self-defense, after all, your life may depend on it!

While it is not our intention here to go into great detail about weapons, as that could easily be the subject matter for another entire book, we feel it is necessary to touch on a few points.

Firearms are likely to be present in nearly any of the 100 million households in America, since there are approximately 225 million handguns known to be on the streets. Most states allow defense of one's home by use of a firearm, and an increasing number permit licensed individuals to carry a handgun outside the home. Legal or not, if you do not have at least 20–25 feet between you and your assailant, you *cannot* reach for your firearm, draw, point, and pull the trigger before he is upon you. This has been proven time and again, even by skilled or "fast draw" marksmen, who were drawing from a holster on a gunbelt. The average citizen who carries a gun for protection carries it in a boot, a leg holster, a purse, or some other "inaccessible" area.

Why do you need 20–25 feet before you should even attempt to use a firearm? Very simple. The average person can move in a forward direction at a rate of 5 feet per ¼ second, or 20 feet per second. You are incapable of reacting to a danger and effectively using a firearm in one second. All you are likely to do is to indicate to your assailant that you have a weapon, which will then probably be taken from you, since he is likely to be bigger and stronger, and which will then be used against you.

Disarming an armed attacker at close range is remarkably easy. Case in point: half of all police officers who die in the line of duty, die by their own handgun which is taken from them during a struggle. These officers are highly skilled in firearms handling and receive specialized firearms retention training not only in the police academy, but at regular in-service training sessions every year. Their firearms still get taken from them and used on them. Let us also point out that many assailants do not have a weapon (nationally only 17% of all rapists had a weapon, according to a recent F.B.I. survey). If you are carrying a gun, or any other weapon that can be readily used by an attacker, you have just increased the odds to 100% likely that there will be a weapon present if you are ever attacked . . . Yours. What can arguably be an asset for protection in your home, where you probably will have more time to prepare a counterattack, can definitely be a liability on the street. *Personal possession of a weapon increases the necessity for early recognition of a dangerous situation.*

If you are considering a firearm for home protection, it is your responsibility to be a responsible gun owner. Be cognizant of the danger to children who might have access to the firearm, and take appropriate measures to insure their safety. There are numerous ways to keep a firearm safe, from trigger guards to state-of-the-art wall vaults which spring open only to a code or your palm print. If you plan to keep the gun unloaded, do not expect to be able to use it in an emergency. You will simply not have the time, or the steady hands, to load it if someone is breaking in, while you are also try-ing to dial 911. Where you keep your handgun will determine not only its accessibility to you in an emergency, but how likely it is that it will be stolen if your house is burglarized. A high percentage of the guns used by criminals on the street have been taken in home burglaries. One place that is <u>not</u> recommended for storing your weapon is under your pillow or next to your bed. Not only is that the place where a thief will first look for a gun, but a sleepy, groggy person who has just been startled and awakened, should never have a deadly weapon immediately at hand. You should be wide awake before you use a weapon that can kill. Many family mem-bers and undoubtedly some family pets have been shot because they were mistaken in the dark for intruders.

Once you decide you are going to own a firearm for home pro-tection, pick a weapon that is easy to use, easy to maintain, is made by a major manufacturer (not a cheap copy — just because it looks similar does <u>not</u> mean it is as reliable), and delivers a "knock down" round. This means that it uses a caliber of ammunition capable of knocking down an assailant with one round fired, as opposed to just puncturing the skin or putting a small hole in him. Revolvers that fall into this category would be 38s and 38 specials, 38–357s, and 44s. Semi-automatics would be 9 and 10 mms, 40 and 45 caliber, and 380s. Our opinion is that the 9mm is marginal. Use of anything that carries a smaller caliber bullet, while certainly capable of killing, will require much greater accuracy and/or more rounds to be fired in order to stop a violent attack.

When deciding between a revolver and a semi-automatic, get someone who really knows firearms to go with you and help you, don't rely on the salesperson. Ideally, any responsible firearms owner *should* practice regularly at the firing range. In general, however, for those who do not spend the time to become proficient with their firearm, a revolver is a better choice because it is a less complex gun than a semi-automatic. Once you learn how a revolver works, you will never forget. There is no on or off button and you can readily tell if it is loaded. Just point and shoot. Semi-automatics can be much more complicated, not only to load, chamber and fire, but also more difficult to maintain. They are more likely to misfire and jam, particularly if the shooter has a weak wrist and cannot apply stiff resistance to the recoil (many women have this problem, as well as a number of men not accustomed to shooting). In the dark, after months of disuse, will you remember if you left the safety off or on and if you push the wrong button will the magazine fall out onto the floor? Unless you are a frequent shooter, a semi-automatic may be a bad choice. Again, seek the advice of experts in your area before making this purchase, and carefully follow the manufacturer's maintenance suggestions.

When it comes to ammunition, there are a couple of things to consider. If you are buying "practice" ammo, reloads, wadcutters or cheap, off-brand bullets are fine, if you don't mind the mess they make and the resultant clean-up. When it comes to purchasing the ammo you intend to use to protect yourself, don't skimp, buy the best — preferably copper-jacketed hollow points. Don't over-buy. Ammunition decomposes over time and should be used up or destroyed once a year and replaced with fresh rounds.

One last word of warning. **Do not use a firearm if you are not ready, willing and able to follow through.** Ask yourself if you are really capable of pulling the trigger and taking another human life. If you are not, don't bluff. The weapon will be taken from you and used on you. You should also be aware that almost half of the burglars currently arrested are juveniles, many under the age of 10. Are they as dangerous as adult burglars? Some definitely are. Are you willing to kill them? You are the only one who can answer those questions, and you had better give it some serious thought before you are faced with such a decision in an emergency.

Chemical sprays for self-protection have been very popular and very lucrative for manufacturers and retailers. Unfortunately they have not been proven to be reliably effective against attackers, and <u>are illegal in some jurisdictions</u>. The active ingredients in these canisters are varying percentages of CN (Chloroacetopheone, commonly known as "Mace"); CS (Orthochlorobenzalmalononitrile, also known as "Military Tear Gas"); or OC (Oleoresin Capsicum, known as "Pepper Spray"). In addition to understanding the varying percentages of several possible active ingredients available, many of which are so minute as to be worthless under any circumstances, one must also be aware of several totally different delivery systems offered in these similar appearing canisters.

Misting or cone mist units emit spray patterns that cover a wide cone shaped area. The sound of the unit being activated may scare off the lesser committed (unlikely), however this misting process is affected by even the slightest breeze, is likely to be blown back into the users face, and is the easiest to defeat due to the minute amount of agent actually being delivered.

Burst or fogger units deliver a large amount of active ingredient and are target friendly. They are more accurate and are less affected by wind conditions than misting units. The sight and sound of the unit being activated is impressive, and may temporarily intimidate a nervous attacker. Burst units, however, deplete their resources quickly and should be replaced after every use. In addition, they would affect everyone in an enclosed area, victims and others alike.

Next we come to the Streamer or "Splatter Streamer" Units. These units deliver, or are *supposed* to deliver, a stream of chemicals which must be focused directly at the eyes of an attacker in order to be effective. While they are not much affected by wind, they must be accurate, as they only affect the respiratory system through the tear ducts. Not only is accurate targeting difficult in a violent confrontation, but ineffective if glasses or any type of eye protection is worn. In addition, they have very short range and must be "walked" in to the appropriate target. They are normally silent when activated.

It would be wonderful if all we had to do was push a button and spray away any assailant. Unfortunately, contrary to advertising claims, these chemicals are highly over-rated. Realize that even police departments that use chemical agents have large "back-up" systems such as batons, firearms, radios to call for help, and usually a trained partner who is similarly armed. In addition, police have a responsibility to attempt to "neutralize the situation" without harming the suspect, if at all possible. You, the citizen, have no such responsibility, and have the right to use whatever legal means are available to you to survive.

While chemical agents may cause temporary eye irritation, some short-term respiratory problems, and general discomfort in a controlled "laboratory" testing situation, the effectiveness of all of these chemicals depends on *pain compliance*. These chemical agents should <u>not</u> be counted upon to *incapacitate*.

Pain compliance can be expected to have some success when the subject is focusing totally on the momentary discomfort. Most assailants in a violent confrontation are under the influence of drugs or alcohol, enraged or excited, goal oriented, and receiving a huge blast of their own adrenalin — they do not *<u>usually</u>* feel pain! They *can*, however, be *incapacitated,* but not by a chemical agent that even manufacturers have been forced to admit will not take effect, under ideal circumstances, for several seconds up to three minutes. A great deal can happen in three minutes with a violent attacker that can still see you and harm you, even if his eyes are beginning to water. We will soon discuss more efficient ways of *incapacitating* an attackers vision.

The danger with chemical sprays is not their limited usefulness. The better ones can be *helpful* as an *additional* self defense tool to be used *in conjunction with* effective fighting skills. While they cannot be counted on for a sole source of instantaneous defense, nor will they be effective against an <u>armed</u> assailant, they can begin to work in your favor after several minutes, if the struggle is still going on. Just be certain you have a self-defense plan that will allow you to survive for those first few critical moments before the chemicals begin to take some effect. Also be aware that the shelf-life of many of these chemicals is limited, some to as little as six to eight months before deterioration of the active ingredients begins. They are adversely affected by heat and cold as well, which will accelerate their deterioration. Obviously, if these agents have been stored in a warehouse, or in someone's vehicle, or been sitting on a shelf for a substantial period of time, they would not be a wise purchase. Look for dated materials and attempt to determine length and type of storage.

Some of the more amusing and ridiculous "repellent" devices marketed recently are the color or paint sprays to squirt on assailants and the "odor ampules" which supposedly make you smell so bad that no one will attack you.

First of all, we fail to see how turning someone green or purple, even if those are not their favorite colors, is going to physically stop them from an assault. Now it might be helpful to the police, because if they see a "green guy" running down the street they would probably realize he might have done something he shouldn't have. . . of course, you're dead or wounded and it's of little help to you!

As for bad smells preventing even the most personal attacks such as sexual assaults and rape, well, homeless women on the streets of America are raped all the time (and they don't bathe often). Women who have been running, excercising and working in their yards get raped. Moreover, this type of device tends to perpetuate the myth that if you smell good, or look good, you are contributing to your own downfall. Nothing could be further from the truth. You are not selected as a rape victim because you are overwhelmingly attractive to the rapist. Elizabeth Kennedy, Executive Director of American Women's Self Defense Association recently remarked regarding these "skunk oil" devices: "This reminds me of the ridiculous suggestion, still promoted today by some self defense instructors: urinate or defecate on yourself and the rapist will not want to rape you! Can you urinate and defecate on command? It's hard enough to go in the cup when the doctor asks. . . imagine trying to do that in a life and death situation!" Furthermore, I wouldn't bet my life that such an act would have the slightest deterrent effect on a rapist.

Stun guns are devices designed to deliver an electrical "shock" to a potential attacker, temporarily immobilizing him, and allowing escape by the victim. These are not legal in all jurisdictions and have several drawbacks. First of all, it appears in early test results that they are not as effective when used on a man as they are on a woman. Individuals who regularly are exposed to electricity such as welders, plumbers, auto mechanics and electricians are less affected, and some have little or no reaction to being shocked. Also, the attacker is usually bigger and stronger than his victim, and is able to wrestle the device from them and use it on them. Your self-defense plan is worthless if you are flopping around on the ground like a fish out of water!

In order to be effective, under ideal circumstances (which never occur on the street), it is necessary to "reach out and touch someone" with the charged device, preferably chest level, <u>and hold it there for three to five seconds</u>. Few attackers, even if they have never seen such a device, are going to stand still and let you poke them with anything for that long. Again, you have reaction time to consider, assuming you were not expecting the attack and did not have the device in your hand, charged and ready for use when you realized you were going to be assaulted. Remember how long it takes for a person 20 feet away to reach you — one second! The odds are simply against this scenario working out in your favor. If you are going to have to make contact with someone as they are charging you, wouldn't it make more sense to be going for a vital target that is going to incapacitate them, without the liability of a weapon that can be used on you? Retailers rarely tell you about the <u>down</u> side of a product they wish to sell to you.

Tasers are similar devices, not widely distributed and not legal in all jurisdictions, which are generally gun-like in shape and appearance, and which shoot charged electrodes on retractable wires which are supposed to attach to the attacker and "zap" him. While these do give you a bit of distance between you and your attacker, they have the same limitations and liabilities. This was the type of device used in the L.A.P.D. incident with Rodney King. Everyone who viewed this widely seen video saw Mr. King rise again and again after being "shocked". Not only is this an example of its limited effectiveness, but should be a caution regarding civil liabilities if used by mistake.

Knives of any size or type, regardless of whether they are legal, evoke one single response from all self-defense experts: _Don't use them!_ Knives can be taken from you and even turned on you while still in your hand. Knife wounds are generally the most lethal and if a knife is not present at the outset of a confrontation, do not introduce one.

A 3½ to 5 inch knife wound to the heart or stomach can cause instantaneous unconsciousness and death. If the skin above the Subclavian or Carotid arteries is cut 1½ to 2½ inches, unconsciousness can occur in 2 to 5 seconds, with death following in less than 12 seconds. The Radial and Brachial arteries require only ¼ to ½ inch deep cuts to produce loss of consciousness in 14 to 30 seconds and death in 1½–2 minutes. In addition, these are frequently inner-arm "defense wounds" inflicted on a victim who is attempting to protect his or her face and upper body with arms raised, and have the additional liability of causing immediate impaired use of fingers, hands and arms.

With most bullet wounds, the injured tissue tends to quickly close up, coagulate and seal around the injury. A knife wound causes a gaping injury that opens up and cannot seal itself, as every movement repeatedly tears it open. It usually must be surgically closed. Are all knife wounds lethal? No, but they all usually produce a great deal of bleeding, the substantial chance of infection, and are all potentially dangerous. Defense against attackers armed with knives will be discussed in the section on Self Defense Theory.

There are hundreds of miscellaneous gismos and gadgets on the market touted as self-defense equipment including "key-cats" (a pointed metal device that protrudes through the fingers of the wearer), brass knuckles, weighted gloves, "slappers" (ask an "old" cop about these), expandable batons, heavy flashlights designed to double as weapons, etc. In each case, you must ask yourself several questions before purchasing and using these items:

~ Is it legal in my jurisdiction?

~ What are its limitations and drawbacks?

~ Can it easily be taken from me and/or used against me?

~ Will the observance of this weapon by an assailant increase his violence towards me? (because he believes that I will try to hurt him)

~ Will it be readily available if I am attacked?

~ How much skill does it take to use effectively?

Realize that before any weapon can be used in the majority of all violent confrontations, it will be necessary for you to physically defend yourself and gain the advantage over your assailant. Most attacks begin within 12 feet of the victim; not enough time to effectively use most commercial weapons. Enough time, however to institute defensive and offensive physical moves which will be discussed shortly.

CHAPTER THREE

SELF DEFENSE THEORY

Natural Weapons

*C*ontrary to some popular beliefs, it is not necessary to *kill* an assailant in order to protect yourself. While death may be a possible, eventual result of the self-defense actions you take against an attacker, it may not occur soon enough to benefit you. Lethal moves, in and of themselves, are generally not the most efficient ways to stop a fight immediately.

Simply because someone has received a fatal injury does not necessarily mean that they will instantly drop over dead. We call it the "Charging Bear Theory". If the continuing momentum of a charging 1200 lb. bear causes him to fall on you and crush you to death, it won't matter much that he eventually died from the wounds inflicted upon him. Veteran police officers tell of many incidents where violent criminals continued their vicious attacks even after being shot repeatedly and receiving mortal injuries.

The objective of your successful counter-attack should be to immediately prevent your attacker from continuing his assault. You must think of your assailant as a mechanical man (or woman) that must be disassembled or *incapacitated* in such a manner that it can no longer harm you. Neither pain nor potentially fatal injuries can be counted on to accomplish this goal quickly enough to preclude further injuries to you, even though your assailant is mortally wounded.

How, then, can we accomplish this incapacitation? What injuries *will* stop a fight, or at least give the victim a serious advantage? Where are these *vital targets*, and how can they be attacked effectively? Consider three important little words: *vision, wind,* and *limbs*. Incapacitation of any one or more of these areas will stop or seriously impede the fighting ability of anyone, instantly! If your assailant can't see, can't breathe, can't use his arms or legs, then it isn't going to be much of a fight. This can all be accomplished in the first few seconds of a confrontation, without any weapons at all, except those you were born with.

First, let's discuss what our natural weapons are, and then how to use them. Working our way down from top to bottom, your head is an excellent and often overlooked weapon. When we say "use your head", we don't necessarily mean your brain. The top of your head is an excellent battering ram. Children seem to know instinctively that if they "head butt" another child in the stomach, they will win the playground fight because the other child will have the wind knocked out of him and not be able to fight. This works effectively for adults too, particularly when the victim is smaller, and it is an unexpected mode of attack. It can be improved upon, however. While your assailant is bent over from the strike to his stomach, quickly raise your head up under his chin, causing a forceful uppercut, driving him backwards and possibly causing him to bite through his tongue. (Illustrations 3a and 3b)

Your forehead (frontal bone) and upper back of your head (parietal bone) are also excellent weapons to strike with. These are hard, bony structures of the cranium and there is little danger that you will sustain a serious injury from pounding your forehead into an assailants chest or breastbone, or from slamming the back of your head into his face, chest, or collarbone. You can, however, expect to cause injuries to your attacker from these actions. Continuous pounding on the chest in the area of the heart can cause an erratic heart beat, and possibly lead to an attack. Head strikes to the sternum (breastbone) can break it and cause difficulty breathing. A broken collarbone will incapacitate an arm, and many facial injuries can also adversely affect breathing (such as a broken nose). These injuries can all be accomplished with just your head. (Illustrations 3c and 3d)

The next natural weapons we will discuss are your hands. Your hands are capable of punching, poking, pinching, scratching, chopping, grabbing and slapping. In general, we do not recommend punching with your fist unless you are a trained boxer. An untrained individual is very likely going to break bones in their hand or wrist with the first strike to someone's jaw. These injuries are called "Boxer's breaks" and are very common. A much safer, and equally powerful, punch is a *palm strike*. This is delivered with fingers curved slightly and palm extended toward the strike surface. The strongest strike is at a 45 degree angle, with joints lined up (wrist, elbow, shoulder) in a straight line. (Illustration 3e). Round-house punches do not generally deliver the power of a "straight shot". Care should be taken with any barehanded strike to the face to avoid teeth which may cut and penetrate your skin. Any mixing of body fluids such as saliva and blood can be sufficient to infect with life threatening diseases such as H.I.V. (AIDS) and Hepatitis B. This is also why we do not recommend *biting* your assailant, except as a last resort.

Poking, pinching, scratching, grabbing and slapping are pretty self explanatory, and specific targets will be discussed later in this segment. Scratching would not be one of the most desirable attack choices because of the possibility of infection from resulting blood contacting any open wounds on your hands, even injuries as insignificant as paper cuts. Chopping uses the knife edge of your hand and little finger.

The next natural weapon to be considered would be your elbows and forearms. To call the use of these weapons "elbow strikes" is probably a misnomer, because you are not actually using your elbow as the strike surface. A forearm strike utilizes the fleshy area between the elbow and wrist that is exposed when one "grabs" an imaginary peg in the center of their chest (thumb to chest), swiveling their shoulder solidly toward a target.

Unlike a thrown punch which requires noticeable preparation, this strike is an effective surprise strike that is difficult to block. A rear "elbow" strike utilizes the fleshy area immediately above the elbow and is most powerful when the elbow is kept close to the ribs, and the shoulders and hips are engaged to drive the blow straight back to the attackers ribs or solar plexus. (Illustrations 3f and 3g)

Your knees are also excellent weapons. Your targets may vary depending on the position of your assailant. As you will see when we discuss targets, the groin is not the only location for an effective knee strike, and may not be as successful as one might hope. Because many assailants expect this type of assault by their intended victim, and therefore try to take some evasive action to protect their groin, a "fake" to the groin with a knee, swiftly finished instead by a kick to the *knee* of the assailant, may cause an incapacitating injury. (Illustrations 3h and 3i)

Now let us consider our feet as weapons. Feet are good for kicking, scraping and stomping. In addition to kicking a kneecap in the direction it was not intended to bend, and scraping down the shinbone, stomps to the instep of the foot are very effective. Even a bare foot stomp can break the small, fragile bones on the back of the hand or on top of the foot. A stomp to the Achilles tendon is a "take out" action. These targets will be discussed in more detail shortly. (Illustrations 3j and 3k)

It would be very rare in most confrontational situations for all of your natural weapons to be rendered useless. Even if your arms are pinned, for example, your feet, head, and knees are still free and usable. A thorough understanding of these natural weapons along with a knowledge of incapacitating vital targets (i.e. those affecting vision, wind and limbs) on your assailant will provide you with the means to survive and win most confrontations. This leads us to a discussion of specific vital targets.

ILLUS. 3A

Demonstration of "head-butt" technique

ILLUS. 3B

ILLUS. 3C

Demonstration of "head-strike" to sternum or chest

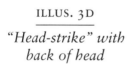

ILLUS. 3D

"Head-strike" with back of head

ILLUS. 3E

"Palm strike"
technique

ILLUS. 3F

Demonstration of
"forearm strike"

ILLUS. 3G

"Rear elbow strike"

ILLUS. 3H

1 of 2

"Fake" to groin

ILLUS. 3I

2 of 2

*Follow-up with
kick to knee*

ILLUS. 3J

*Stomp to Achilles
heel*

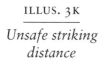

ILLUS. 3K

Unsafe striking distance

ILLUS. 3L

Safer "protected" position

Vital Targets

While actual fighting techniques and maneuvers should be taught in a hands-on, classroom situation, there are a few critical principles that can be discussed here, that may save your life in an street fight. First of all, assuming no weapons are present, you cannot attack *vital targets* from a distance. You cannot protect yourself from an experienced fighter at arms length. A boxer or kick-boxer needs that distance to power their strikes. You must quickly get very close (yes, chest to chest) to reduce the power of a punch, protect *your* vital targets, and to reach targets that will effectively incapacitate your assailant. (Illustrations 3k and 3l)

While you may be queasy about sticking your fingers in someone's eyes, if your life, or the lives of your loved ones, are at stake, get over it! It is a very effective way of stopping a fight very quickly. If the bad guy can't see you, he can't find you to hurt you. Even if glasses or a mask are present, the eyes are accessible. Your target should actually be the cheekbones, with the fingers of both hands aiming upwards at a 45 degree angle. If you aim directly at the eyes and your assailant instinctively ducks or recoils evasively, your jab may only strike eyebrows. The eyes, however, are set deep in the skull and as your fingers aim upwards from the cheekbones, (underneath glasses, if present) they will automatically plunge into the eye sockets. This is not considered a lethal move, nor is the injury always unrepairable, but it is an effective fight stopper.

Wind, or breathing ability, can be affected in a number of ways. Obviously, if an individual cannot breathe properly, he cannot sustain an effective assault. One of the easiest targets is perhaps the windpipe, or trachea, itself. No one wears steel collars, and it is usually easily accessible. Again, your fingers do the work. You will not be able to get a fist into this area, however, your fingers poked hard into this spot, or a chop (with fingers together and outside of the little finger slicing into this target) will impede breathing and possibly even crush the windpipe, as it is quite fragile. Obstruction of this airway causes asphyxiation. Even relatively gentle pressure in this area causes breathing difficulties and extreme discomfort.

Breathing difficulties are produced in several other ways. A broken collarbone (from a downward chop across the clavicle), or a broken breastbone (sternum) from a solid strike can cause jagged bone fragments to protrude into the upper lobes of the lungs, impeding breathing ability. A roundhouse punch under the arm of an assailant or an upward palm strike to the lower rib area can drive splinters into the lower lobes of the lungs. (One of the very few times a "roundhouse" punch is suggested). A punch to the solar plexus can also, temporarily, cause loss of breath. A broken nose, while not a serious injury or an immediate fight-stopper, will cause the individual to "mouth-breathe" and keep him from sustaining rigorous activity. It may also cause blood to flow down the back of his throat, further hampering breathing.

Incapacitating injuries affecting the use of limbs include broken collar bones, arms, elbows, wrists, hands, knees, legs, feet, ankles. Surprisingly, since the inner ear contains the organs of balance and equilibrium, a punctured eardrum can cause inability to restore the body to an upright position, in addition to nausea, vomiting and other symptoms, obviously rendering the individual powerless to pursue their intended victim.

A solid blow to the kidneys, on the back, generally above the beltline and on either side of the spine, will usually cause the knees to buckle, cause general weakness in the legs and can cause death up to several days after the injury.

To put it very simply, *all that it takes to win a fight is successfully using your natural weapons against your opponents vital targets and natural weaknesses, as the opportunity permits during the course of any fight.* The following diagram (*Primary Targets and Physical Weaknesses of the Human Body*) and accompanying key, illustrates the location of such targets and denotes the likely incapacitating results upon injury.

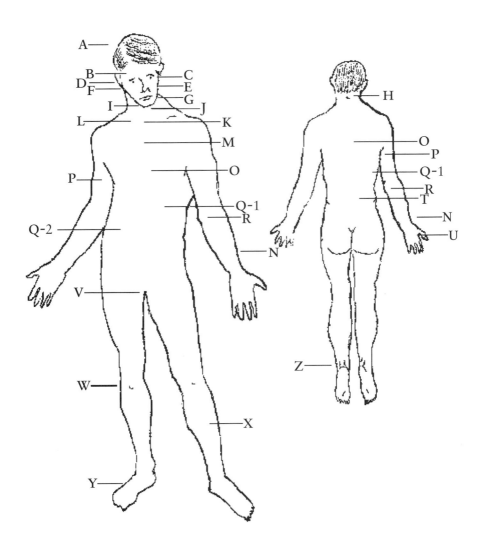

Diagram 3–1

Primary Targets and Physical Weaknesses of the Human Body

Key to Primary Targets and Physical Weaknesses of the Human Body*

A   Hair. A secondary target often used to pull someone off balance, expose a primary target, such as the throat, or to distract opponent.

B   Temple. A blow to the temple can cause unconsciousness, and even death, particularly if the head is immobilized on the opposite temple.

C   Eyes. A primary target which can incapacitate an assailant. If he can't see you, he can't find you to hurt you.

D   Ears. An incapacitating injury if eardrum is punctured, causing loss of equilibrium and balance.

E   Nose. A broken nose is generally not an injury that will stop a fight, however, it will cause the recipient to "mouth breathe", which will shorten the amount of time he can fight effectively.

F-1 Jaw at the "Condyloid process", where the jaw hinges just under the ear. This is the weakest point, and the easiest to break. Could be lethal if broken bone punctures the adjacent carotid artery. A broken jaw alone, however, is not necessarily a "take out" or incapacitating injury. (F-2) Mandibular Angle. A soft area and sensitive pressure point just above the jaw hinge and below the ear. Inward and downward pressure causes moderate to high levels of pain and loss of balance. (See Diagram 3-3 on page 46)

G   Mouth. Not an ideal target with bare hands, as teeth can puncture skin and mix body fluids of assailant and victim. Additionally, broken teeth and split lips are not physically "take out" or incapacitating moves, however they might be "psychologically" incapacitating moves under certain circumstances.

H   The notch at the hairline on the back of the neck. A blow to this area can cause a wide range of injuries from temporary to permanent paralysis, loss of many autonomic responses, and death. Not normally an easy target to reach during a confrontation.

I   Chin. Often a natural target of a palm strike or fist. Not generally an effective fight stopper, but can be used to expose a primary target such as the throat, solar plexus or groin, and to propel opponent backwards, perhaps into another assailant.

J   Windpipe or walls of the trachea (throat area) . A primary target which, if incapacitated, is a take out move. The windpipe is very fragile, and collapses with little pressure. If someone cannot breathe, they cannot fight. A crushed trachea could be lethal.

K   Jugular Notch. The notch just on top of the sternum in the center of the lower neck, where the right and left collarbones meet. Inward and downward pressure causes low to high levels of pain, involuntary cough reflex, loss of balance, will cause attacker to back away. *Expect some initial resistance* to the pain. Deep penetration into the throat can block airway and cause inability to breath.

L   Collarbone or Clavicle. A primary target, downward strikes with as little as six pounds of pressure can break collarbones. This incapacitates the arm involved and severely restricts use of the other. This is usually a fight stopper and is normally associated with a great deal of pain. (See Diagram 3-4 on page 46, showing collarbones, breastbone and ribs.)

M   Sternum, or Breastbone. The sternum, if cracked or broken (possibly accomplished with a headstrike), can cause slivers of bone to penetrate the lungs and impede breathing ability. If this injury does not stop a fight, it will undoubtedly slow it down.

N   Radial Pressure Point. A normally very sensitive area which runs from approximately the inside of the wrist to just below the inside of the elbow. Often used for temporary pain compliance and to relax the grip of an assailant. *Requires practice to accurately locate.*

O   Heart. The heart is approximately the same distance from the front as it is from the back. Continuous pounding on the chest or the back can produce an erratic heartbeat. *Obviously, any serious interruption of the heart function can be lethal.*

P   Lymph Nodes. Located in the armpit, a serious injury here will incapacitate the arm, possibly permanently. Normally not possible with bare hands, and heavy clothing makes an attack on this area relatively unsuccessful.

Q-1   True Ribs - upper seven pair which fasten to sternum. When these ribs are broken from a blow to the side, splinters can lodge in the lungs and impede breathing. In addition, broken ribs are extremely painful. This injury can be incapacitating, *but cannot always be counted upon to be an immediate fight stopper.*

Q-2   False Ribs - lower five pair of ribs which do not attach to the sternum directly. The lower two pair of these do not attach at all and are called "floating ribs". These floating ribs can be broken rather easily by an upward palm strike. A painful injury which impedes breathing. Identifying the exact area during a violent confrontation may be tricky, especially when concealed by layers of clothing.

R   Elbow. Since it only bends one way and is extremely sensitive, it can be used to control and direct body movements. Requires some practice, but can be very effective when used for "armbars", take downs, and control situations. The arm breaks relatively easily at this point when outstretched, with a sharp blow directly to the elbow area. A broken arm, obviously, would be likely to stop or severely limit the ability of an attacker to harm you.

S   Solar plexus. The stomach is a good target for a head butt. If contact is made, the wind is knocked out of the opponent and/or he may be pushed off balance. If contact is avoided by "sucking in" the stomach, a secondary target (the chin) is exposed for an upward thrust by the head. This doesn't take great expertise to execute and is surprisingly unexpected by the opponent.

T   Kidneys. Located just above the beltline and on either side of the spine, a solid blow will usually take the legs out from under the person being struck. Can give the victim several seconds to escape or execute additional counterattack. Kidney injuries can be lethal, but are not necessarily immediate take-out moves in a fight.

U   Back of Hand. The bones here are very fragile and break very easily. Swelling occurs very rapidly and can incapacitate, or at least impede, movement. Grabbing and holding functions become impaired, using a weapon with that hand may also be difficult or impossible. This is a good disabling move which is not lethal.

V   Groin. A common target, however one with *only about a 30% chance of incapacitation.* Males learn at an early age to protect this area, to expect this type of attack, and offenders often wear cups or groin protectors for that reason. Pelvic injuries to males or females are very painful and can be incapacitating, at least temporarily. An initial attack to this area would be less likely to be successful than one instigated later during the course of the fight, when the opponent was not prepared to defend the area.

W   Kneecap. The knee, like the elbow, only bends one way, and is a weak point in the strongest limb. A blow to the knee can be immediately incapacitating and is a primary target in a fight. If an individual cannot walk, he cannot pursue you.

X   Shin. A sensitive and vulnerable area on the front of the lower leg which can be scraped or kicked, causing moderate pain. Not a take out move in a violent confrontation, but effective in combination with a kick to the knee and a foot stomp.

Y   Instep. The arched upper part of the foot. Like the bones on the back of the hand, these bones are very fragile and break easily. This area is a primary target for a foot stomp, being relatively unprotected even inside a shoe or boot. Immediate pain and swelling can cause inability to walk or run effectively, giving a distinct advantage to the other side.

Z   Achilles Tendon. Incapacitation of this area is a take out move and is a serious, sometimes permanently disabling, injury.

*These targets are by no means the only vulnerable areas of the human body, however they are the ones most likely to be exposed during a violent confrontation.

The Most Lethal Targets for Knife Wounds

No.	Artery or Location	Size	Depth Below Surface	Consciousness Lost in Seconds	Death
1	Brachial	Medium	½"	14	1½ Min.
2	Radial	Small	¼"	30	2 Min.
3	Carotid	Large	1½"	5	12 Sec.
4	Subclavian	Large	2½"	2	3½ Sec.
5	(Heart)		3½"	Can be instantaneous depending on depth of cut.	
6	(Stomach)		5"		

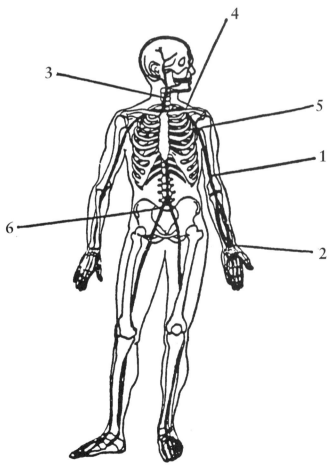

Diagram 3–2

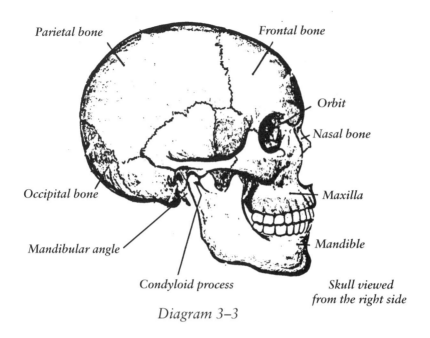

Parietal bone

Frontal bone

Orbit

Nasal bone

Occipital bone

Maxilla

Mandibular angle

Mandible

Condyloid process

Skull viewed
from the right side

Diagram 3–3

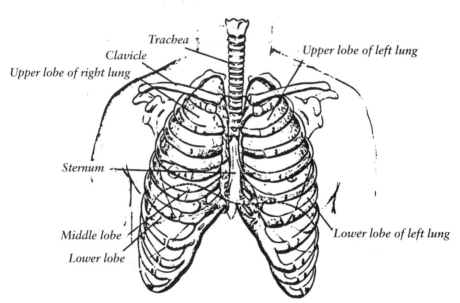

Trachea

Clavicle

Upper lobe of left lung

Upper lobe of right lung

Sternum

Middle lobe

Lower lobe

Lower lobe of left lung

Diagram 3–4

*Projection of the lungs and trachea in relation to the rib cage
and clavicles. Dotted line indicates location of the diaphragm
at the end of an expired breath.*

Formulating a Defense Plan

*T*he information relative to natural weapons and physical weaknesses, together with the suggestions for crime prevention and utilizing survival instincts should begin to give you some ideas for viable self defense plans. It is essential that everyone develop their own plans because we each have different vulnerabilities and risks in our daily lives. You are responsible for determining when and where you are at risk and who might be a threat to you.

While every situation is different and no one response fits all confrontations, a *menu* of defense options should be mentally prepared. No one can be expected to suddenly formulate an appropriate action plan to violent behavior if they wait until the moment they are confronted with it. However, if a variety of self protective responses have been previously considered, while not under duress, an almost instinctive reaction is very likely. Just like fire drills in school, if you know what to do in an emergency, you are less likely to panic, and more likely to survive.

Begin by imagining what you would do if someone attempted to rob or carjack you in a parking lot or garage. Think about whether there is a weapon involved, or multiple attackers. Are you alone or with children or friends? Can anyone else see you or hear you? How far away from a safe, crowded place are you? What if they want you, as well as your possessions? If you decide to fight them, how will you do it? What is your first move and will it be a take out move or a defense move? Does it expose any vital targets? Are your vital targets protected? Remember, for every action, there is a reaction. Every time you cause someone's body to move or react, you may be exposing a target, which gives you another opportunity to attack with one of your natural weapons. Be certain that you protect your vital targets as you fight.

Next visualize what you would do if someone broke into your house while you were: a) sleeping; b) baby-sitting; c) taking a shower; d) in the kitchen, possibly separated from your children. Your response will vary depending on the circumstances such as number of attackers, location of entry, availability of escape or weapon use, etc. Think about it until you are comfortable with your choices. Failure to consider an unpleasant or frightening situation will result in no preparation for defense should it ever occur. It is better to be prepared.

While there is no way to consider all the possibilities for violent confrontations, recognition of the potential for victimization by a criminal element in your daily life, and a knowledge of your strengths, weaknesses, natural weapons and vital targets will prepare you to deal effectively with most situations you may encounter.

In the coming chapters we will be discussing specific risk groups, such as children, teens, women and senior citizens, and the crimes most likely to be committed against them. As you gather more information in these areas, you can add more details to your defense plan. We will also deal with some of the more frequent violent crimes, including robberies, rapes and workplace violence incidents and give you a better understanding of how to prevent and/or survive such confrontations.

Consider this: A criminal usually has a plan, and experience executing it. If, between you and your attacker, there is only one plan – *his* – what do you think will happen? Remember the old adage, "If you fail to plan, you plan to fail". Your life may depend on it.

CHAPTER FOUR

A PARENTS GUIDE TO CHILD SAFETY

Crime Trends Affecting Juveniles

*T*he children of this, or any, nation are its most valuable resource. We should be willing to go to great lengths to protect, nurture and educate them to become stable, contributing members of society. Unfortunately, we are not born with the skills and knowledge to do this. We must learn from someone else, or face the serious risks and consequences of only learning from experience. You would not expect to drive a vehicle for the first time without assistance or training and not make a mistake. You would not automatically be able to drive an 18-wheel truck with 13 plus gears or a large bus simply because you knew how to drive a passenger vehicle. Many parents, however, undertake what is probably one of the world's most difficult jobs without receiving any training or education - how to raise a child and keep it safe, not only from accidents and injuries, but from human predators.

Children are not born with an Owners Use Manual. We tend to "parent" in the manner in which we were "parented". Even if we had excellent parents, however, they did not have to contend with the accelerated criminal activity that now exists. They did not have to worry, as today's parents do, about drugs, weapons, juvenile crime, gangs, drive-by shootings and child molesters, all of which are probably present on a daily basis in the schools *our* children attend, and these are just a portion of the current parental concerns. Many of the activities we may have pursued in relative safety when we were children are no longer harmless and risk-free for the youth of today.

In order to protect your children properly from today's criminal element, it is necessary to recognize and understand the existing dangers in their world. Only then can you adequately attempt to set safe parameters for their activities and help them develop good safety habits.

The object of this section is: 1) to enable parents to keep children safe at home, at a friend's house, at school, sporting events, or when playing or enjoying any recreational pursuits; 2) to help parents *and children* better understand todays risks and dangers and prepare them to *work together* to deal with those situations in a manner that increases safety and survival of the child; and 3) To set forth reasonable rules and guidelines that can accomplish these goals, and to teach the child effective, defensive resistance techniques.

Let's start with some of the most recent information available, as of this writing, compiled from the U.S. Department of Justice, the F.B.I., Bureau of Justice Statistics, and numerous victim-witness centers across the U.S.

There are currently approximately 11 million violent crimes reported every year in the U.S. (remember, only 38% of all violent crimes are ever reported). Of those, at least 23% of the victims are juveniles. This means that 1 in every 13 children is a victim of violent crime. This is nearly a 25% increase since 1987. Many of these crimes take place in or around schools. As early as 1994 it was reported that every school day:

* 14,000 students are attacked;
* 2,600 teachers are assaulted;
* 160,000 children skip school because of fear;

In addition:

* 12% of high school students carry a gun to school, and for every gun there are seven knives;
* More than 13% of high school seniors nationwide have been threatened with a weapon at school;
* More than 3000 school-age children were killed by firearms in 1993;
* Every 5 hours a juvenile is arrested for a violent crime;
* More than 5000 murders and manslaughters were committed by juveniles in 1993, with homicide arrest rates for juveniles more than doubling between 1985 and

1992. During this period, juvenile arrests for weapons law violations increased 62%;

* In 1991 a 12-year-old was at greater risk of being a victim of a violent crime (i.e., murder, forcible rape, robbery, aggravated assault, or simple assault) than anyone above the age of 23;

* The risk of violent victimization for a 17-year-old in 1991 was about double that faced by a 29-year-old;

* As of this writing, *in Los Angeles alone,* there are approximately 1,135 separate juvenile gangs known to be in existence, with an estimated membership of well over 200,000. Accurate nationwide estimates are not yet available.

* The amount of crime just *one gang* can produce is staggering. For example, 7% percent of the youths in Los Angeles commit 70% of the juvenile crimes;

* The average life expectancy for a gang member is 19 years of age. (normal life expectancy in the United States is presently about 82 years of age).

These patterns of increased violence by juveniles is frightening, particularly in light of the fact that the size of that age group has shrunk over the past twenty years. The baby bust is giving way to a new population surge! Based on birth records, by the year 2005, the 15–19 year old age group is projected to increase by nearly 25%.

The October 1993 National Crime Victimization Survey published by the Department of Justice, Bureau of Justice Statistics, states that while victimization rates for personal crimes have declined for most age groups, the *violent* crime rate for young people has been steadily increasing. (See Illustration 4-a).

In addition to the aforementioned violent victimizations, parents also need to be aware of these additional concerns:

* There are over a half-million reported sexual assaults against children every year;

* Sexual misconduct is the principle reason reported for the revocation of teaching licenses;

* Kidnappers are most often driven by sexual impulse;

* The average child molester attacks 300 - 400 children during his lifetime —wherever there are children, there are child molesters. This includes school facilities and playgrounds, sports and recreational activities and child care functions, just to name a few.

* At least 10% of those participating in a home computer on-line bulletin board are looking for sex with a child. They may pose as another child, ask for a name, address and phone number or want to meet in person somewhere.

Recent studies indicate that child molesters are *five times* more likely to become repeat offenders than any other type of criminal. As a result, some states now have laws requiring convicted child molesters to register their address after they leave prison, and this information is made available to the general public. In some cases, neighbors are even notified directly. Most pedophiles, however, upon release from prison (usually after ridiculously short sentences), quietly integrate into neighborhoods full of children without anyone knowing or suspecting their dark proclivities.

Two to three hundred children fall prey annually to the kinds of abductions most commonly in the news, i.e. those committed by strangers, over some period of time and distance, and possibly involving a ransom note or murder, according to the National Center for Missing and Exploited Children. Adam Walsh, Polly Klaus, Roxie Mosier, Morgan Nicks and even the Lindbergh baby are all well-publicized examples of this type of abduction, although the circumstances of each case are different.

When the definition of abduction is broadened to include shorter-term abductions, the number jumps to 3200–4600 a year according to a Justice Dept. report.

Teenagers and girls are the most common victims of stranger abductions. Approximately half the victims are 12 or older and three-quarters of the victims are girls. Two-thirds involve sexual assault, with a majority of victims being abducted from the street.

Black male teens have the highest violent victimization rates

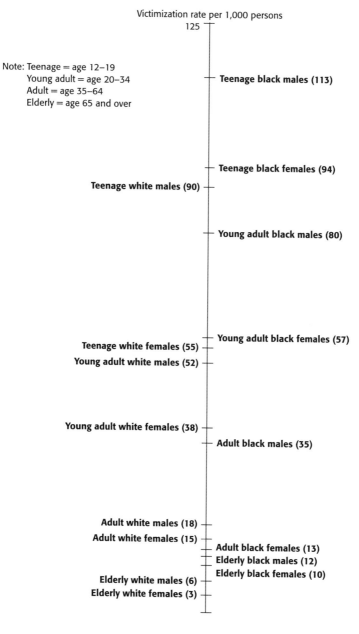

Victimization rate per 1,000 persons

125

Note: Teenage = age 12–19
   Young adult = age 20–34
   Adult = age 35–64
   Elderly = age 65 and over

Teenage black males (113)

Teenage black females (94)
Teenage white males (90)

Young adult black males (80)

Young adult black females (57)
Teenage white females (55)
Young adult white males (52)

Young adult white females (38)
Adult black males (35)

Adult white males (18)
Adult white females (15)
Adult black females (13)
Elderly black males (12)
Elderly black females (10)
Elderly white males (6)
Elderly white females (3)

Diagram 4–1a

Statistics from Bureau of Justice Statistics "Highlights from 20 years of Surveying Crime Victims," October, 1993, p. 20.

Personal theft rates are highest for teenagers and young adults

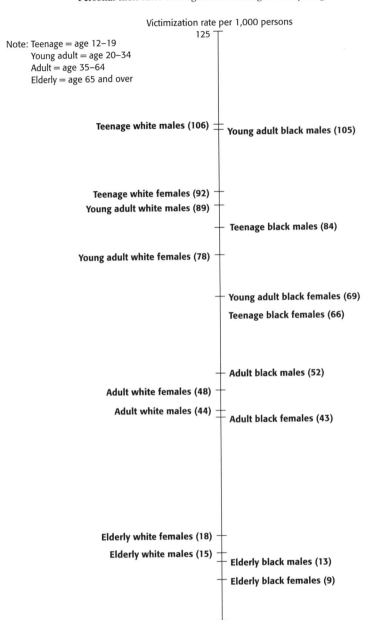

Victimization rate per 1,000 persons

Note: Teenage = age 12–19
      Young adult = age 20–34
      Adult = age 35–64
      Elderly = age 65 and over

Diagram 4–1b

Statistics from Bureau of Justice Statistics "Highlights from 20 years of Surveying Crime Victims," October, 1993, p. 20.

Over 85 percent of these abductions involve force, and over 75 percent involve a weapon. A large number of *attempted* stranger abductions are reported. Most of these consist of an attempt by a passing motorist to lure a child into a car. According to police reports, *children seem to have a large number of encounters with strangers where an abduction is threatened.*

The overall estimate for children currently missing in America is 1.5 million. Lost and runaway children make up the largest portion of that, followed by those abducted by family members and kids whose caretakers tell them to leave, turn them away, or otherwise make no effort at recovery ("thrownaways"). The smallest subset of the missing children are the children abducted by strangers. However, one must add to this figure the incidences of abuse, injury and murder that so many children suffer at the hands of family members in their own homes.

Most of the family abductions are perpetrated by men, noncustodial fathers, and father figures. Most victims are children from ages 2 to 11, with slightly more at younger ages, but relatively few infants and older teens. Half involve unauthorized takings, mostly from the children's homes; the other half involve failures to return the child after an authorized visit or stay. The most common times for family abductions seem to be in January and August. These are the times when school vacations end and visitations are exchanged. In a recent study by the Department of Justice, the period immediately after a divorce was *not* when most family abductions occurred. Instead, 41 percent occurred before the relationship ended. Another 41 percent did not occur until 2 or more years after a divorce or separation.

While every parent's worst nightmare is the fear of a stranger-abduction, the likelihood of such is about as great as getting struck by lightening. It could happen, however it is much more likely that a child will be enticed or seduced into a relationship by a molester known to them or their family. The good news is that an estimated 114,600 abduction attempts are averted each year. Some parents have equipped their children with personal beepers or alarms and given their children special instruction in child safety and self-defense.

Ten Safety Rules for Children

T alk openly with your children about the dangers they may face and the fears they undoubtedly have. Too many times parents have no idea that their children are afraid or worried about something. Fear is often the result of ignorance, and can be alleviated by discussion and education. Children, just like adults, fear the unknown and things they believe they cannot control. Empower your children by teaching them how to recognize a potentially dangerous situation, how to avoid it if possible, and how to successfully deal with it if necessary. Let them exert some control over their own destiny. After all, whenever you are not with them, *they are responsible for their own safety!*

There is one definition that needs to be clarified at the very beginning of any discussion about child safety or anti-abduction techniques. That is, "What is a <u>Stranger</u>"? We always tell children not to talk to strangers, to be wary of strangers, to never leave with a stranger or let a stranger touch them. But if you ask ten children the definition of a "stranger", you will get ten different answers. How can *they* be expected to make that determination without a clear, constant understanding of exactly who and what a stranger is?

The problem is solved with the following explanation: <u>A "Stranger" is *anyone* who does *not* reside in your house, *if* your parent or guardian is not present!</u> This means that, absent a custodial adult, relatives, neighbors, teachers, coaches, friends of the family, and acquaintances, as well as previously unknown individuals, are to be considered strangers when the child is alone with them. This is quite reasonable, given the fact that most attacks on children are perpetrated by people they know. This takes the guess work out of the decision a child must make in order to protect him or herself. They should always be "on guard" when they are alone with *anyone*, other than their immediate family — and there are, of course, exceptions to this, if an abusive relationship exists.

Go over the following rules with your child, making sure that he or she understands that these are for *safety* purposes, *not* control.

1. *Never go anywhere without checking first with your parents or the adult responsible for your immediate care (such as a baby sitter, teacher or coach). Tell them where you are going, how you will get there, who will be going with you, and when you will return.* This information is essential if the child doesn't arrive at its destination or does not return when expected. It gives the police the necessary information to begin a search. Tell your children not to change plans after arriving at their destination without letting you, or their adult guardian, know of the change. A person who means your child harm is less likely to hurt them if they know someone is aware they are with this child and may be monitoring their activities.

2. *Know your exact address and phone number, and know how to call 911 (if available in your area) from any phone for help from police, the fire department, or for an ambulance. This call will be automatically, immediately traced to your exact location and is only to be used in an <u>emergency</u> situation. If you are lost, look for a uniform or someone in charge.* Many children who have moved frequently do not know their address or phone number. Police cannot find parents in an emergency if the child does not know this information. Explain that a "uniform" does not necessarily mean a police officer. Employees in retail stores, restaurants, hotels and movie theatres to name just a few examples, usually wear a type of uniform or have a name tag that designates them as an employee for a specific business. It is usually safer to go to these people for help when they are on duty at their place of employment than to go to a customer or passerby. In addition, be sure your child knows that coins are <u>not</u> necessary when a pay phone is used to call 911. Make certain, however, that your child understands why he or she should <u>never</u> make crank 911 calls. Not only could it cost the life of someone else who needs the police for a *real* emergency, but it could unnecessarily endanger the patrol officer who is rushing to a false alarm.

3. *Always get permission from your parents before getting into a car or leaving with <u>anyone</u> — even an acquaintance, and then*

only if that person knows your <u>codeword</u>*. Never tell anyone your secret codeword.* Pick a simple codeword with your child and make a pact that neither of you will tell anyone what it is, except in an extreme emergency. For example, if a non-custodial parent, or a relative or acquaintance attempts to pick up a child from school, the burden is not on the child to decide whether to go with them or not. If they do not know the secret codeword, the child knows <u>not</u> to leave with them. If a stranger tells your child you have been involved in an accident and taken to the hospital, and you have asked him to bring your child to your bedside, if he doesn't know the codeword your child will know he is lying. Keep the codeword simple and change it if it is ever used or if you have reason to believe others may know what it is.

4. *Never change plans or accept money, gifts, food, drink or drugs without your parents' knowledge and permission.* Make certain your child understands that you don't get something for nothing, and that offers of this nature always come with a price tag. Sexual favors are usually one of the expected paybacks. If it is a legitimate offer, (for example, $10.00 payment offered for clean-up or simple yard work) there should be no reason why the child's parents are not informed and their permission sought first. Other common ploys are: a) getting a child to help them "find" a (non-existent) lost pet or child; b) asking for directions; c) saying they are "talent scouts" or "agents" working for a motion picture company, theatrical agency or modeling studio; d) pretending to be sick or hurt in order to solicit a child's sympathy and cooperation. Tell your child that if someone makes such an offer to them, they should tell you immediately or tell a teacher, the police, or someone in charge. They should make sure a responsible adult knows about it. This may avert repeat attempts at abduction for your child, and save other families from heartbreak. If they believe that an individual is truly in need of medical assistance, they should not go near the person, but go to a <u>safe</u> phone (not inside the person's home or car) and call 911.

5. *Use the "buddy system" whenever possible, and stay with other people for safety. There is strength in numbers. A criminal needs privacy —don't give it to him (or her).* Encourage your child to always play and walk to their destinations with a friend. Children alone are always more of a target for potential predators. Teach them to walk on the sidewalk the *opposite* direction of traffic, (*facing* it, not with it) so no one can slip up behind them in a vehicle without them being aware of it. Tell them to avoid dense shrubbery and dark alleys or deserted areas. Even if they have to wait a few minutes sometimes to go somewhere with a friend, rather than starting off by themselves, it is worth the extra wait for the added safety. (Remember this, Parents, if your child is a little later getting home from school or events because he or she waited for a "slow" friend.)

6. *Never let a stranger (even one in a uniform, unless you have called the police) into the house when you are alone, and never tell someone on the phone or on a computer what your address is, or that you are, or will be, alone.* Your child should not assume that simply because an unsolicited individual is in a uniform indicating that he is a police officer, fireman, plumber, phone repairman, or an employee of a public utility, etc., that it is necessarily true. *Anyone* can obtain these uniforms (*and badges*) from a uniform supply shop with no questions asked, and criminals often do just that. If in doubt, the child should be instructed to call 911 and ask if they can verify the identity of the caller requesting entry to their residence while they are alone. Tell them that if they speak to this individual at the door, they should always do so through a closed, locked door. If the stranger tells them there is an emergency such as a fire, gas leak, approaching flood or tornado, if they do not already know this to be true, they can determine the truth about any such emergency with 911 operators.

The first thing a child should do if they answer the phone, *before* giving out *any* information, is to ask who is calling. If they do not recognize the voice, regardless of who they *say* they are, they should get their parents or guardian to talk to them. If their parents are not home, they should tell the caller that "they are busy" and ask to take a message, getting a return phone number and <u>writing it down</u>. <u>They should **never** tell a stranger that their parents aren't home!</u> Sometimes a caller may ask them their address or when their parents will be back. They should tell them, "My Mom can't come to the phone right now", or "My Dad's busy right now and I can't help you. Please call back later." That's all they have to say. <u>Then hang up!</u> Further discussion is pointless and can only cause them to get confused and blurt out information they didn't want to reveal. They do not have to talk to a pushy, rude person who continues to pry information out of them, no matter who they are. If you have an answering machine, it can allow them to screen incoming calls and save them from having to talk to anyone they do not know when you are gone.

Occasionally they may receive a call which is harassing, threatening or obscene. They may get calls from someone who says nothing, but stays on the line and breathes heavily. When this happens, tell them to gently hang up the phone and not re-answer it for a period of time or until you get home. Tell them not to say anything back to this individual, not to slam the receiver down or yell or blow a whistle or give <u>any noticeable reaction</u>. People who do this sort of thing do it to get a response out of their victims — any response. If they don't get one, it's not fun for them and they tend to stop bothering those people. Many phones are equipped with caller identification mechanisms now, which helps alleviate some of these problems. Problem callers are beginning to learn that they can be caught and punished more easily now.

If you have a computer at home, or your child uses one at school or at a friends house, and/or has access to any of the on-line public bulletin boards or "chat" lines, you need to carefully monitor these communications. Not only is extremely raunchy pornographic material readily accessible to anyone traveling the currently unregulated information highway, but experts now agree that at least 10% of those utilizing these bulletin boards are looking for sex with children. They often pose as another child and ask for personal information, offer gifts, and want to meet somewhere with the children they correspond with. Warn your children that they may not be communicating with another child and to never give out their full name, home address or phone number to anyone they talk with on-line. Above all, they should <u>never</u> agree to meet with this person without parents present.

7. *You do <u>not</u> have to be polite to a stranger when you are alone with them. Keep strangers outside of your "intimate circle" (at least two full arms lengths away). Say "No! I don't know you! Get away from me!", if someone tries to touch you in a manner that frightens or confuses you, or makes you uncomfortable. Immediately tell a responsible, trusted adult and/or the police what happened. Don't stop telling until you feel certain this person will not come near you again.* Parents should give their children <u>permission</u> to be rude to strangers when they (the parents) are not present to protect them. This includes relatives and family friends (remember the definition of "a stranger"). Don't tell them they must be polite and let Uncle Harry or Aunt Matilda kiss them and fondle them when you are not there, or even if you <u>are</u> present, if it makes them uncomfortable. Children should have the right to refuse unwanted physical affection from <u>anyone.</u> Being forced to accept unwanted advances as a child may set them up for a lifetime of physical and emotional abuse. Remember, it is your <u>child's</u> safety and well-being that you should be protecting first and foremost, not the "sensitive feelings" of an adult who should also be more concerned about the child than themselves.

When a "stranger" is alone with them, a child should keep them outside their "intimate circle". If an actual danger or threat is perceived, that distance should be increased by backing away, telling the adult to back off or calling for another individual to help them. Tell them to trust their instincts. If they feel uncomfortable, act on those feelings. It is better to be safe and possibly over-react in such a situation, than to be afraid of hurting someone's feelings and do nothing to avert a possible assault, or worse. They do not have to be "nice" to someone who is making them feel bad. If they allow the behavior once, it will continue and probably escalate.

It is never too soon to discuss "good touches" and "bad touches" with your child. It is *your* job to be sure they understand what is and *is not* acceptable touching. Just because it may be a bit uncomfortable for you to talk about it, don't assume they automatically know, or that they will learn at school or from friends, what is okay and what is not. One easy way to "delicately" explain it to a very young child is to tell them that they should not be touched anywhere their bathing suit touches them. With the brevity of today's bathing suits, that should not be excessively restrictive. The use of an anatomically correct doll is also an option. Use the real, proper names for body parts, not "cutesy" baby names. If your children ever *are* the victim of a molester, and are unable to adequately describe and testify to where they were touched or hurt, a predator may go free.

8. *It is never a child's fault if someone molests them or touches them improperly. Do not keep silent about such touches, even if you are told to keep it a secret, or you are threatened in any way if you tell. It is OK to physically resist such touches, with force, if necessary.* It is not the fault of the victim if someone else makes a decision to do something wrong or criminal, and there should be no guilt associated with such victimizations, especially when the victim is a child. It is, however, important for children to try to make certain that the *opportunity* for such actions is rare or non-existent, and that they can often exert a great deal of control over the circumstances. Remember what we discussed about providing a bad person with uninterrupted privacy. Your child should be advised to stay with friends, in crowded public areas, or inside your own locked home. Tell your child that no one should ever touch them on the intimate parts of their body except a physician, with a parent and a nurse present, during a medical examination. Any other touching of this nature should be resisted forcefully and they should tell and keep telling until

they feel safe again, and the offending person is removed from any contact with them.

9. *Trust your feelings and instincts, and run <u>away</u> from danger — to a <u>crowded</u> place. Communicate with grown-ups about problems that are too complicated for you to handle on your own. Most adults are good people who care about you, truly have your best interests at heart, and will believe in you and help you.* Emphasize that a child should not run to a poorly lit, unpopulated area, but rather to a busy, crowded place. If they are not near a mall or business, they should go to a residence that appears occupied and summon the occupant. They should stay on the porch (these people are strangers, after all) and ask them to call the police. In a dire emergency, they could throw a rock or heavy object through a window if they must, in order to get attention, if the resident is reluctant to come to the door to help them.

10. *You should never feel that it is too late to ask for help. You are special and deserve protection from harm. Keep asking until you receive help and feel safe again.* In reality, lots of people care about children, even if they don't know them, and have a natural desire to protect them. Your child should know that *most* people are good citizens — only about 7% of the population is responsible for the crime in our country.

Effective Anti-Abduction Techniques for Younger Children

Most children under the age of about 10 or 12 do not need *complicated* self-defense training. Fancy footwork and mock battles with a sparing partner who will not deliberately hurt them will do little good in a real confrontation. Besides, the more difficult and numerous the techniques are, the more likely they are to forget them in an emergency. The type of confrontational situations they are most likely to face can normally be thwarted with a few simple, easy to remember moves, an understanding of how to use their "natural" weapons, and attention-getting verbalizations.

Before teaching children any technique that can hurt or injure another person, be sure they understand that these actions are *only* to be used in an emergency, and *never* used to show off or "horse around" with friends or acquaintances. If, however, they *must* hurt someone in order to survive unharmed, give them your permission, in advance, to do so.

Review the natural weapons and vital targets discussed in Chapter 3 with your child, to the extent that their age and maturity will allow thorough understanding, giving special attention to the effective use of the following:

~ Head (head butts and strikes) - (See Illustrations 4a-c)

~ Fingers (jabs to the eyes, pinches, grabs to the groin)

~ Palm strikes

~ Elbows (forearm strikes and rear elbow strikes)

~ Knees

~ Feet (snap kicks, scrapes and stomps)

Children are very effective, enthusiastic fighters once they understand what they are capable of doing, and are rarely reluctant to use these potentially injurious methods to protect themselves. *Adults* are often much more conservative in their approach to the use of force, because a) society has repeatedly taught them it is wrong to hurt another person; b) if you injure another person they may sue you; c) the result of the potential injury may freak them out or sicken them (i.e. using your fingers to poke into someone else's eyes). Children do not have these hang-ups yet, as a rule, and therefore see things much more simply, enabling them to act without undue and often unnecessary reflection of the consequences of their actions. This is beneficial when children are young, more vulnerable to attack, and less likely to perceive the danger in advance.

A simple resistance technique they should be taught is a move we call the **propeller**. This action would be employed if a would-be assailant attempted to grab them by the hand, wrist or arm. Since the *thumb* is the key to the strength of any grip, it is easily defeated by the child vigorously swinging the limb being held around in a circular fashion, front to back or back to front, imitating the course of a propeller on a plane, helicopter or motor boat. (See illustrations 4d and 4e.)

Another effective anti-abduction technique is called **running in place**. This involves the entire body and can be implemented anytime a child is picked up off the ground by someone who is attempting to carry them off. The legs and arms should begin working vigorously in tandem, as though the child was actually running, which will put fists, elbows, knees and feet into play, continuously striking the would-be abductor. This makes it nearly impossible for anyone to hang on to the child without sustaining painful injuries, regardless of whether they are trying to pick the child up from the front, back, in a fireman's lift or bridal carry. In addition, if being picked up from the front or back, the child can used their head to smash into the assailants face or chest. (See illustrations 4f to 4j).

This maneuver will probably cause the assailant to drop the child, so a brief discussion is in order about how to fall with the chin tucked in to keep the back of the head from striking the ground. In addition, holding the arms straight out to break a fall can cause fractures of the arms and wrists, so a landing on the forearms or buttocks would be preferable. This is one area where beginning martial arts training can be beneficial, in that a great deal of time is given to learning how to fall properly early in the training process.

We mentioned finger jabs and groin grabs briefly earlier in this section. Point out to your child that if they grab, head-butt or kick the groin area, or kick or stomp a knee, shin, or foot of an assailant, it is natural for the attacker to bend down to grab the injured area. This will probably place their eyes within jabbing range of even a small child. This makes for a good "double-whammy", enabling the child to run to safety. (See Illustrations 4k-l).

If a child is the victim of an abduction or molestation attempt, it is not only important that they resist physically, but verbally and loudly as well. If, however, they do not yell something significant that causes anyone who might overhear to take notice, it will not do them much good. We can scarcely go anyplace in public anymore without hearing a protesting child, being made to do something they don't want to do, or whining because they can't have their way about something. We have learned to thank our lucky stars it is not *our* child causing the commotion, and to ponder whether the long-suffering parent ever spanks for bad behavior! We rarely pay much attention to a child yelling "No! I don't want to go!", or crying "Leave me alone!". If, however, we were to hear a child yell **"No! *I don't know you!* Get away from me!"**, we would probably take notice, and wonder whether this adult had any right to control this child. We might either get involved personally to help the child, notify a police officer or person in charge. At the very *least* we would pay attention and be able to recall the events if a witness should eventually be needed. A child is very unlikely, no matter how angry they are at a parent or guardian, to say the words "I don't know you!", which is why it strikes a cord when they are uttered.

ILLUS. 4A

1 of 3

Starting position for "head butt" technique

ILLUS. 4B

2 of 3

Elbows raised, head rammed into stomach or groin

ILLUS. 4C

3 of 3

*Back of head then
slammed up under
chin of attacker*

Demonstration of "Propeller"

Arm is swung in clockwise or counterclockwise direction, breaking grip of assailant

ILLUS. 4F

*Anti-abduction
technique
"Running in
place"*

ILLUS. 4G

*"Running in
place" with
"head strike"
to face of
assailant*

ILLUS. 4H

Same technique from "Fireman's lift"

ILLUS. 4I

"Running in place" technique from "bridal carry"

ILLUS. 4J

"Forearm strike" from face to face pick up

ILLUS. 4K

1 of 2

"Foot stomp"
or "kick" to
shin

ILLUS. 4L

2 of 2

Follow-up with
"finger-jab" to
eyes when
assailant grabs
injured limb

Safety Guidelines for Parents

Parents must establish a cooperative effort with their children for maximum safety. You cannot be by your child's side 100% of the time, but you can instill certain values and standards by which your child can make educated decisions about his or her own personal safety. The following suggestions can aid in this regard.

1. *Always know where your child is, who he/she is with, and when they will be home. If they are home alone, be sure they take appropriate security precautions and tell no one they are alone.* If they are to be left at home alone, or are baby-sitting in someone else's home, be sure they are instructed to lock doors and use any security measures that may be present (such as setting perimeter alarms). If there is an answering machine, let the machine answer incoming calls, or have them use it to screen calls. Don't be "embarrassed" to call and check on them if they are away from home for an extended period of time. Be stern if they are not where they said they would be. Know who your children's friends are.

2. *Be sure your young child knows his/her address, phone number and the 911 function, if available in your area, or how to reach police, fire and ambulance response teams.* At home you can place a 3 x 5 index card next to the phone with pertinent emergency phone numbers, including poison control and/or hospital help-line numbers. In a real emergency, you can never find a phone book or a needed number fast enough.

3. *Discuss appropriate behavior with strangers, both in and out of your presence, and develop a codeword that only you and your child know.* Explain that bad guys (and gals) are not always bad looking or scary, and may not even be strangers. Discuss what a normal safe distance should be from strangers ("intimate circle"). Tell your child never to approach someone in a car and never leave with anyone who does not know the codeword (the exception would, of course, be a *uniformed* police officer in a

marked police unit or a fireman in an extreme emergency, i.e. natural disaster, bomb threat, fire, etc.).

4. *Play "what if" games with your young child to determine their scope of understanding of dangerous situations.* For example, "What if a person showed you a picture of a cute little puppy, told you it was lost, and asked if you would help them look for it, what would you do?" What if they stated that it was a baby that was missing? See what response your child gives. Ask them what they would do if someone was trying to get into the house when they were home alone? Don't assume they understand what to do in these situations, make sure they know how to handle them.

5. *Do not provide your children with "personalized" clothing with their names on it, i.e. belts, shirts, ball-caps, etc.* This unnecessarily targets your child and allows a stranger to call them by name and create a false intimacy. <u>Notice if someone is paying undue attention to your child!</u>

6. *Don't make discussion of body parts taboo.* Discuss "good touches" and "bad touches", allowing a frank conversation. Tell your child to trust his/her instincts about whether a situation is appropriate or not. Listen to your children. It may be difficult for a child to explain if someone has done something to them that they didn't like and don't understand. Never belittle any fear or concern your child has, real or imaginary. Keep the lines of communication open and active. Tell them to run <u>from</u> danger <u>to</u> a crowded place. A child molester needs *uninterrupted privacy* — be sure your child doesn't give it to them.

7. *A <u>polite</u> child may not be a <u>safe</u> child. Give your child permission to be rude, even physically forceful, if necessary, with someone who forces their attention on them when you are not present to protect them.* Teach or reinforce your child's knowledge of vital targets and appropriate actions if they must fight. Tell them they have your permission to scream, yell, use physical force, and immediately tell on anyone who threatens them in any way.

8. *Tell your child what to do if they are ever lost, separated from you, and/or have an emergency.* If they cannot get to a phone, tell them to look for a uniform or someone in charge. Teach them to be resourceful and to take responsibility for their own safety when you are not around. Encourage the "buddy system".

9. *Always accompany your children to a Public Restroom and never leave children alone in a car.* Do not depend on others to watch your children, they are <u>your</u> responsibility.

10. *Monitor your child's home computer time.* On-line Bulletin Boards can contain pornographic, sexually explicit material, and child molesters use them to attract and communicate with potential victims.

11. *Statistically, nearly every household in America could have at least one firearm. You may be a responsible gun-owner and have your firearms in a safe place, but your child doesn't always play at home.* Investigate the homes of your child's friends, where your child plays, to determine the security measures in place to protect curious children.

12. *If your child rides a bike, be sure you make him/her aware of local ordinances and traffic laws regarding bike riding and bike safety.* Be sure they know what traffic signals and traffic control signs mean and conscientiously obey them, including proper signaling for turns, lane changes and stops, so a motorist can anticipate their actions. In a confrontation with a motor vehicle of any type, *<u>the bicycle will lose.</u>*

13. *Have your children fingerprinted and keep the card in a safe place along with a current photo and a detailed description including any scars, birthmarks, traits, etc.)* Update the photo at least annually. In an emergency, this information is needed quickly and should be prepared in advance, when you are thinking calmly, not when you are frantic with worry. Most police stations and/or sheriff's departments will provide fingerprinting for your children.

CHAPTER FIVE

SEXUAL ASSAULTS — WHAT EVERY WOMAN NEEDS TO KNOW

N ationwide, there is a *reported* forcible rape every 5 minutes. In 1995, 2 out of every 1000 women 12 or older reported being raped. Most experts now agree that for every rape that is reported, eight to ten more have occurred and gone unreported. Rape is the most under-reported violent crime in America. There are a multitude of reasons why so many women choose not to report the crime, from embarrassment at public disclosure and mistrust of the result of criminal proceedings, to fear of reprisal from the assailant. Since many women are now in management positions, supervising male subordinates, reporting such a personal violation may be perceived to adversely affect their position or upward mobility within the corporate world. It is not our intent to critique the reasons why this crime is so under-reported, but rather seek to keep it from happening at all, and enable women to successfully thwart the criminal who attempts to molest them.

In order to reduce the likelihood of such an assault, it is helpful to know *when, where, how* and *why* most of these attacks occur, and *who* is most likely to attempt such a crime. As for the question of *when* a sexual attack is most likely, July and August are usually the months that show the highest number of attacks reported. Any time the weather is hot, however, the risk is high. Obviously, if the weather is fair and warm, more "victims" will be outside and accessible, more homes will have open windows and doors for fresh air, car windows will be rolled down, etc. In addition, it is useful to be aware that almost two-thirds of all rapes occur at night, between 6:00 PM and Midnight.

Remember, however, that regardless of the odds, rape attempts occur anytime the opportunity exists, day or night, hot or cold.

Let's talk about *where* rapes are most likely to occur.

* Approximately 77% take place indoors. Of those, 90% happened at private residences, 6% at motels, 1% at schools, and 3% at places of business.

* 57% take place in the *victims* home, 20% in the
  assailants home.
* 10% take place in cars, 13% outdoors.

How rapists behave and how they accomplish their crimes
varies greatly from criminal to criminal, but each individual rapist
usually conforms to his own specific pattern or M.O. (method of
operation) each time he seeks a victim. Remember that rape is a
serial crime for which rehabilitation efforts have been shown to
have little or no effect on future behavior. Extensive surveys of victims indicate the following:

* 2 in 10 completed rapes involved assailants who stalked
  their victims before they assaulted them.
* 3 in 4 men used physical force to rape their victims;
  1 in 4 used threats, alcohol, drugs, or subterfuge to
  gain compliance.
* Studies suggest that when a women is raped and complies
  with her attacker, it is often because she is too drunk or
  high at the time and she is being raped by someone whom
  she knows and had previously trusted.
* Nationwide, only 15% of all rapists showed a weapon.
* In almost 8 in 10 rapes, one offender confronted one victim,
  however multiple attacker situations among teens is on the
  increase.

Why anyone would choose to harm another individual is
impossible for the average citizen to fathom. We do know, however, that the primary motivation is power, intimidation, and often
deep-seated anger at the opposite sex (and sometimes same sex),
not overwhelming sexual attraction. That undoubtedly accounts
for attacks against infants and elderly women who have done nothing to "tempt" these cretins. As a matter of fact, the assailant is
often unable to complete the act of intercourse, and, as a result,
often becomes increasingly violent with his victim.

We also know that a rapist normally does not select a victim
that he believes could or would do him harm or fight back effectively (another reason for selecting helpless children and weak-
appearing individuals). The rapist does not expect to be hurt. The

element of surprise is a big factor in favor of a potential victim who fights back effectively! You are never too old, too young, too unattractive or too well protected to be a target. This is a crime of violence (normally) directed at a female. Sex is the *tool*, or *instrument* of violence, <u>not</u> the *goal*. The goal is utter domination, humiliation and subjugation, sometimes resulting in the death of the victim.

The ability to identify *who* might be a threat can sometimes make the difference between becoming a statistic or avoiding a sexual attack. Although it is not possible to read someone's mind, the following statistics can be helpful in determining whether to be alone with an individual or not:

* Almost 80% of all rapists are *well-known* acquaintances, and another 10% are familiar individuals, and known to the victim;
* Only 10% of all rapists are total strangers;
* The *most violent* rapists were either total strangers or intimates (meaning current and former spouses and/or boyfriends);
* Rape victims who knew their offenders were just as likely to be injured as victims of strangers;
* Offenders and victims were most likely to be of the same race and same age. (This does not apply to Child Molesters.)

Additional information and profiles of the four main types of rapists (A. power– reassurance, B. power – manhood asserting, C. anger – punishing, and D. sadistic enjoyment) will follow in the next section.

Since nearly 90% of all rapists are known to the victim, we must be concerned about what "the media" like to call "date-rape". This is a misleading and somewhat insulting term which usually implies that it wasn't a "real" rape, and that the victim teased or encouraged or in some way contributed to her own downfall. This couldn't be farther from the truth. If you went out on a date and were murdered, would it be called "date-murder"? A better term would be "acquaintance-rape", because that is what it really is. These are <u>real</u> rapes, with <u>real</u> force and violence. No one is to blame except the rapist. No one else made him step over the line between civility and consent, and animalistic force. "No" means **NO!** and should be respected. Whether you are a dating adult, or a parent of a teenager who is dating, this is a matter that concerns you. The best guess by experts is that at least 50% of all rapes occur in a dating situation. Adults as well as teens are always safer if they double-date or stay in a crowded place. Never let your friends abandon you with someone in order for them to be alone. Insist that they either stay with you or take you home first. If they won't, call a cab, a friend, or if necessary the police.

If your date is bossy and overbearing and insists on ordering for you, encouraging you to drink or partake of drugs, isn't ready to take you home when you ask, dominates the decisions on where you go, etc., then he is not interested in how you feel or what you want or need, and certainly not your safety. He is probably not going to take "No!" for an answer. As a parent, if your daughter's boyfriend is telling her what to wear, who to have as a friend, how to wear her makeup or hair, then you have reason to be concerned. If you see signs of bruises that your child brushes off without proper explanations, she may be in an abusive relationship and not know how to get out of it. You may have to insist on getting in the middle of it. Estimates are currently surfacing that indicate up to half of all high school relationships are abusive to some extent. This can set the victim up for a lifetime of abuse, since this becomes her only experience with relationships and she believes this is normal. Low self-esteem accounts for many of these situations. <u>No one</u> deserves this type of treatment.

From national statistics we know that the profile of the average rape victim is as follows:

* Under 35 years of age, with the average age of a victim being 15 years of age;
* Single, separated or divorced;
* Lower income category;
* Unemployed, in the Armed Services, or a student (one in every four college girls will be raped before she completes her four years);

* Lives or works in the central city (almost twice as high a risk as living in an urban area);
* Is a renter (risk is over three times that of a homeowner);
* Lives alone, or in a household of 3 or more persons (it is easy to stalk and determine the vulnerability of an individual living alone in a densely populated multiple housing unit with poor security and high visibility. If there are 3 or more living together, odds are that at least one of them is a child, and they tend to "spill their guts" about every bit of personal information they know — you have <u>no secrets</u>, and security is therefore affected adversely.);
* Separated or divorced women were six times more likely to be victims of violent crime than widows, 4½ times more likely than married women;
* Women aged 15 to 24 were 3 times more likely to be raped than other women;
* Women who were separated, divorced or who had never married were *9 times* more likely to be raped than those who were married or widowed.

Does this mean that if you do not fit the profile outlined above, you are not likely to be a victim? <u>*No it does not!*</u> If you are a female, there is at least a 50% chance that you will be a victim of at least one sexual assault during your lifetime, and it is important to always be cautious about allowing anyone to have uninterrupted privacy with you. In addition to the fears of injury, pregnancy or even a violent death from a potential sexual attack, one has to be concerned today with the very real possibility that this individual can infect you with the AIDS virus, or Hepatitis B, and this will adversely affect everyone you care about. In order to save your life, *you may <u>have</u> to fight for it!*

Rapist Typology

The following profiles of the four major types of rapists were primarily compiled in 1994 by Sex Crimes officers of the Tulsa, Oklahoma Police Department and are useful reference tools. These should be used only as *possible indicators* of criminal sexual behavior. Simply because someone fits *some* of the categories does not necessarily mean he is a rapist, but it *does* mean one should exercise caution when alone with this person, until you can be certain of your safety.

A. POWER – REASSURANCE RAPIST

1. **Purpose**
   a. Reassures his manhood.
   b. No intent to hurt/degrade.

2. **Pre-offense behavior**
   a. Fantasizing (predominantly about sex).
   b. Limited planning.

3. **Selection of victim**
   a. Prowling on foot
   b. Voyeurism
   c. Residential area
   d. Victim in residence
   e. Nighttime hours
   f. Intra-racial
   g. Victim is alone
   h. Victim not likely to resist

4. **Victim Evaluation**
   a. Past observations
   b. Uses a surprise approach
   c. Initial victim contact
   d. Wants submissive response

5. **Use of Intimidation**
   a. Threat of a weapon
   b. Weapon of opportunity
   c. Use or display of weapon (for control of victim)
   d. Rare use of profanity
   e. Minimal force used (more for intimidation)

6. **Sexual Behavior**
   a. Unselfish
   b. Has victim remove her clothes
   c. Use of foreplay
   d. Involves the victim
   e. Wants reassuring verbal activity
   f. Does (sexually) only what victim allows

7. **Sexual Dysfunction**
   a. Premature ejaculation
   b. Impotence

8. **Completion of Assault**
   a. Apologetic
   b. Takes a souvenir
   c. Short time with victim

9. **Post Offense Behavior**
   a. Short period between assaults

b. May maintain a diary/journal
c. Will seek a safe haven after
d. Collects soft core pornography
e. Remorseful
f. Never up to his expectations
g. May recontact victim

10. **Profile**
   a. Inadequate
   b. Low self-esteem
   c. Gentle, quiet, shy
   d. Low high school standing
   e. Single, never married
   f. Dates, younger, less attractive
   g. Misdemeanor sex offenses
   h. Pornography user (soft core)
   i. Underachiever
   j. Poor peer interaction (with males also)
   k. Few, if any friends
   l. A Loner
   m. Solitary pastimes, hobbies
   n. Non-athletic, especially team
   o. Nighttime person
   p. Lives alone, with parents
   q. Lives/works in area
   r. Dominant mother
   s. Weak or absent father
   t. Walks to rapes
   u. Menial employment
   v. Poor work history
   w. No personal contact job
   x. Rarely drives
   y. Plain automobile
   z. May have received counseling

B. POWER – MANHOOD ASSERTING RAPIST

1. **Purpose**
   a. Asserting/showing his manhood
   b. Feels he is entitled to it
   c. Expressing his masculinity

2. **Pre-offense Behavior**
   a. No prior planning

3. **Selection of Victim**
   a. A Victim of opportunity
   b. Singles bars
   c. Intra-racial
   d. Evening hours
   e. Same age range as victim
   f. Away from residential/work area

4. **Victim Evaluation**
   a. Con approach
   b. Easy to con victim
   c. May have had previous contact
   d. Lures her to a place to assault

5. **Use of Intimidation**
   a. Use of moderate force
   b. Likely to hit/slap
   c. Uses his physical strength
   d. Weapon of choice (if used)
   e. Profanity

6. **Sexual Behavior**
   a. Selfish behavior

b. No foreplay

c. No attempt to involve victim

d. Tears clothing off victim

e. Victim there to be used

f. Will do whatever he wants (sexually)

g. Vaginal, oral, and anal likely

h. Spends long time with victim

7. **Sexual Dysfunction**

a. Retarded ejaculation

b. May not ejaculate

8. **Completion Of Assault**

a. Threats upon leaving

b. Future problem if reported (he says)

c. May take a trophy

9. **Post-Offense Behavior**

a. No remorse

b. No diary or writing

c. Porno not important

d. Not likely to recontact

e. Likely to assault again

f. Establish an alibi

10. **Profile**

a. Self-centered

b. High self-esteem

c. Described as "macho"

d. Drives a "macho" vehicle

e. "Macho" occupation

f. Smooth with women

g. He breaks relationships

h. Very jealous

i. Very possessive

j. Women do not like him

k. Cannot take criticism

l. Athletic

m. Neat appearance

n. Frequents singles bars

o. Heavy drinker

p. Drunk driving arrests

q. Family fight calls

r. More than one marriage

s. Does not like authority

t. If Veteran—kicked out

u. Problems in high school

v. Arrests for assaults/fighting

w. Arrests for property destruction

x. Father dominant

C. ANGER – PUNISHING RAPIST

1. **Purpose**

a. To Punish for real/imagined wrongs

b. To degrade or humiliate

2. **Pre-Offense Behavior**

a. Stressor in personal life (typically a female)

b. Stressor in work life (typically a female)

c. No prior planning

3. **Selection Of Victim**

a. Usually a spontaneous attack

b. Assailants residence/ work area

c. Victim in wrong place/wrong time

d. May resemble female in personal life

e. Usually same age or older

f. Any time day or night

4. Victim Evaluation
a. No real evaluation
b. Wants almost any female

5. Use Of Intimidation
a. Blitz style of attack
b. Excessive force involved
c. Immediate use of force
d. Profanity and anger obvious
e. Weapon of opportunity

6. Sexual Behavior
a. Selfish behavior
b. Rips/tears clothing off
c. Degrading sex acts
d. Anal followed by fellatio
e. Likes resistance
f. Painful sex acts
g. Any type of sex he wants

7. Sexual Dysfunction
a. Retarded ejaculation

8. Completion of Assault
a. Threats
b. May not say a word

9. Post-Offense Behavior
a. Spends short time with victim
b. Force before/during/after (excessive or brutal)
c. No remorse

10. Profile
a. Outgoing
b. Well liked
c. Above average IQ
d. Some college
e. White collar worker
f. Does not work to potential
g. User of minor drugs
h. No alcohol/drug abuse
i. Triad (firesetting, bed wetting, mutilation of animals)
j. Rigid personality
k. Large dogs (if owns)
l. Outdoorsman
m. No arrest record likely
n. If arrests, white collar type
o. Sadistic, bondage, pornography
p. Detective magazines
q. Nazi, military collector
s. Appears to have a good marriage
t. Family man
u. Drives a family/"official" vehicle
v. Usually vehicle has high mileage
w. Compulsive personality
x. No mental health care
y. If in military, did well
z. Anal intercourse fixation
aa. Anti-social personality

D. SADISTIC ENJOYMENT RAPIST

1. **Purpose**
   a. To inflict pain
   b. Physical pain
   c. Psychological pain

2. **Pre-Offense Behavior**
   a. Premeditated
   b. Well planned
   c. Violent fantasies (sexual)

3. **Selection Of Victim**
   a. Any time of day/night
   b. Known as a cruiser
   c. Could occur anywhere
   d. Victim usually not known
   e. Symbolic age/description
      possible

4. **Victim Evaluation**
   a. Uses con approach
   b. Ability to gain control

5. **Use Of Intimidation**
   a. Weapon likely
   b. Weapon of choice
   c. Violent behavior
   d. Excessive/brutal force
   e. Psychological control
   f. Immobilizes victim
   g. Non-emotional voice

6. **Sexual Behavior**
   a. Selfish behavior
   b. Cuts clothing off victim
   c. Experimental sex
   d. Inserts objects
   e. Prolonged sex acts
   f. Bondage
   g. Torture
   h. Records acts (video, audio,
      Polaroid pictures, etc.)

7. **Sexual Dysfunction**
   a. Retarded ejaculation
   b. Ejaculate on body

8. **Completion Of Assault**
   a. Most likely to kill
   b. All details planned out
   c. Victim(s) immobilized
   d. Victim may be hospitalized
      (if survives)

9. **Post-Offense Behavior**
   a. No remorse
   b. Leaves very little evidence
   c. Protects his identity
   d. Will assault again
   e. Establishes an alibi
   f. No pattern developed

10. **Profile**
   a. Lone wolf
   b. Married with conflict
   c. More than one marriage
   d. High school education at
      best
   e. Hot tempered
   f. Mental health treatment
   g. History of domestic assaults
   h. Alcohol abuser
   i. Impulsive
   j. Self-centered
   k. Manipulates people
   l. Superficial relationship
   m. Porno not important
   n. Contact sports
   o. Labor/action oriented job
   p. Known as a hard worker
   q. Dominant mother
   r. Arrests for fighting/drinking
   s. Domestic assaults

Wrestling the "Office Octopus" or the "Date from Hell"

Not all sexual assaults are of the "violent" or "life-threatening" nature. Many are simple assaults by "handsy" co-workers or overly amorous suitors. Most women can recall instances when someone took advantage of an opportunity to "touch" her or rub up against her "accidentally". These acts usually occur because the perpetrator does not believe that the victim can or will do anything about such a "small transgression". Indeed, many women have been taught that it is improper to even acknowledge that they have been "slimed". Meanwhile, their faces are burning red with embarrassment and disgust. Individuals who prey on women this way must be dealt with directly and firmly, or the behavior will continue and escalate.

While these lesser offenses must be handled with less force by the victim since there is often less actual physical danger to her, they are still unpleasant episodes and the perpetrators should be made *painfully* aware that the action shouldn't be repeated. Often, simply going to a supervisor at work with a complaint about the behavior of a co-worker produces less than satisfactory results, and usually ends up being a "he said - she said" shouting match, particularly if there were no witnesses to the incident. Too frequently the behavior continues because nothing definitive happened to stop it. This is very frustrating and humiliating to the victim.

The following techniques can be used in these situations to quickly and effectively demonstrate your disapproval of the actions of another, and will most likely dissuade this person from a second attempt. There is no need for a discussion with a third party who was not present, since the countermeasures would not have been employed if a serious breach of etiquette with regard to personal assaults had not occurred. No one should feel that they must allow someone, to "paw" them or take unsolicited liberties, even a date, a boss or a supervisor.

The first maneuver can be employed if someone slips an arm around your waist from the side. You can bring your arm up over the outside of their elbow, turning slightly away from them and applying pressure to "hyper-extend" their elbow. (You can drag them to personnel this way if you choose.) (See Illustration 5a - 5b) Exercise caution if you practice this with a friend — a little pressure is very painful!

If an individual places their arm around your shoulders, you can bring your arm up and over the back of their upper arm and across your body in a downward "slam dunk" type of motion. While they are "kissing" the floor, you can explain to them that you don't appreciate their attempts to fondle you. (See Illustrations 5c - 5d).

Unsolicited "bear hugs" from someone you are *not* having a relationship with are totally out of line. If your arms are free, you can grasp an elbow and pull yourself around into a position for a rear elbow strike to the jaw. (See Illustration 5e). If your arms *are* pinned, bend your knees and turn towards your assailant while dropping the shoulder closest to him. Now you can execute a very effective elbow strike to the groin. (See Illustrations 5f - 5g).

Another typical act of "familiarity" is the "shoulder or back rub" attempt. This can be thwarted by raising either arm and swiftly turning in the direction of the raised arm, which will go over both arms of the individual and wrap them up tightly. This will effectively and uncomfortably trap his arms. Speed and the element of surprise are important tools for this technique. (See Illustrations 5h - 5i).

A "full nelson" is a wrestling technique that should _never_ be a part of even consensual horseplay. (See Illustration 5j). Not only can consciousness be lost, but other injuries such as shoulder dislocations can occur. If an attempt is made to place you in such a hold, it can be defeated *prior* to the hands being locked behind your head, by simply raising one shoulder and lowering the other. A "nelson" requires equal pressure to be applied with both hands, and that cannot be accomplished if one shoulder is higher than the other. (See Illustration 5k).

A similarly inappropriate action from any friend or associate would be a head lock. If this should occur, first turn your head to avoid a fist in your face as shown in Illustration 5l. Then wrap your arms around the legs (below the knees) of your assailant and lean towards him as you lift slightly. He will fall *hard* to the ground. (See Illustration 5m).

Occasionally an unacceptable "grope" will occur on a dance floor. It really isn't necessary to endanger other dancers by slamming your date to the ground, however a variation of the "finger lock" technique might be just the ticket. Slide your hand up so that your fingers are over his. Then, grasping tightly, bring them down and back as shown in Illustrations 5n and 5o until you have the desired "control" over your date.

For more serious transgressions from someone who won't leave you alone or threatens you in some way at a club or party when you have a drink in your hand, the following suggestion will allow you to escape and get help. First pour the drink into his lap, then, when he looks down, shove the drink container into his face. If the container is glass, this can cause serious injury, so this technique should only be used for serious assaults, or if you believe you are in imminent danger. (See 5p - 5q).

ILLUS. 5A

1 of 2

Technique for unwanted arm around waist

ILLUS. 5B

2 of 2

Applying upward pressure to elbow or distal end of arm

ILLUS. 5C

1 of 2

Technique for unwanted arm around shoulders

ILLUS. 5D

2 of 2

Rolling your bicep up over the back of their upper arm, keeping your back straight, "slam-dunking" them across your body

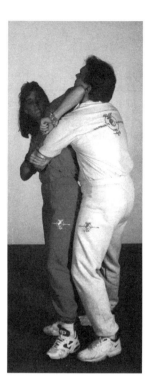

ILLUS. 5E
***
*Rear elbow
strike from
"Bear Hug'
with arms free*

ILLUS. 5F AND 5G
***
*Release and groin strike from
"Bear Hug" with arms pinned*

*Forced release
from hands on
shoulders*

ILLUS. 5J
_____
Full nelson

ILLUS. 5K
_____
Defeating full nelson

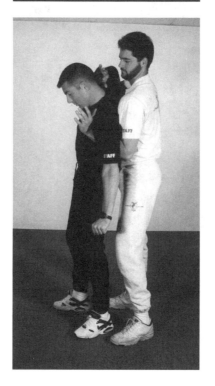

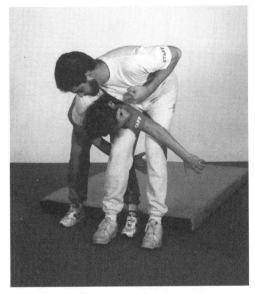

*Defense for
"Head Lock"*

ILLUS. 5N

1 of 2

*Demonstration of
"finger-lock"*

ILLUS. 5O

2 of 2

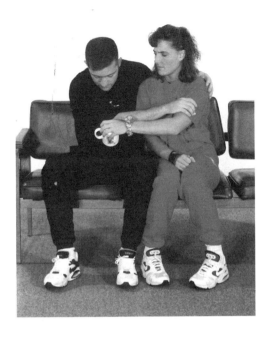

ILLUS. 5P

1 of 2

First, dump drink in lap of offender

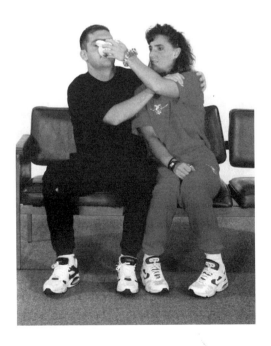

ILLUS. 5Q

2 of 2

As he looks down at lap, bring drink container up into his face.

Groundfighting for Women and Girls

Most fights and virtually all rapes eventually go to the ground. Most victims believe that once they have fallen or been knocked to the ground they have been defeated and are now defenseless, or at a distinct disadvantage. <u>Nothing could be further from the truth!</u>

One of the most effective fighting positions, and the hardest to penetrate by an attacker, is on the ground, on your back. This is the preferred fighting position for many police officers and other experienced street fighters in violent confrontations not involving a firearm. It allows you to protect *your* vital targets while aggressively attacking your assailant's weaknesses if they continue to approach you. It also confuses many offenders who are used to "stand-up" fights, and, since they have no plan for this type of victim response, you have the surprise advantage.

Particularly when inferior size and strength are factors, groundfighting is a good choice. We look to the animal world for examples of effective fighting techniques by creatures that are often smaller and weaker than their predators. Squirrels, rabbits, cats, groundhogs, ferrets, and even hamsters all fight on their backs. Remember the last time you tried to pick up a rabbit or cat that didn't want to be picked up? In spite of the fact that you are at least 10 to 20 times the size of these animals, I'll bet *they* won the battle! Even other primates such as monkeys, marmosets, gorillas and baboons, to name just a few, all fight on their backs.

If you watch young children in a playground or nursery school you will probably see that fighting and wrestling on the ground is instinctive for humans too, until adults intervene and "civilize" the children's behavior. Most parents can recall an incident or two in a *very* public place when their children displayed their burgeoning independence in just such a manner, and while they attempted to retrieve the youngster from the ground, may have been the victim of a well-placed kick or two. The problem is that most parents train their children *not* to do this, rather than *when* to do it.

Now that you are a "socially conscious" adult, in order to help you overcome your fear of falling or of being on the ground, let us point out certain facts. If you are on the ground, your attacker has to come to *you*, and when he does so, he will unavoidably expose himself to an effective, damaging attack. If you are smaller than your attacker, this helps equalize the size differential — everyone is the same height when they are laying on the ground! You now have *four* limbs to fight with instead of only two, including the *longest* and *strongest,* your <u>legs</u>. (Proper groundfighting position is demonstrated in Illustration 5r). Even a child or very short person's legs are usually longer than a tall person's arms, and are strong enough to keep the attacker at bay. (Illustration 5s) As he comes close to you, you have access to many incapacitating vital targets, (See Illustration 5t) from the knees and shins to the face and throat. You also have the ability to use a scissor throw technique to bring your assailant to the ground by placing one foot low on the inside of the attacker's leg, and the other one just below knee level, and rolling toward the inside foot, keeping knees slightly apart. (See Illustrations 5u - 5v)

If an attempt is made to stomp or kick you, grab the foot and sharply twist it towards the other leg. (See Illustration 5w) If one of your feet is captured, quickly pull it into your body while kicking out at the face or throat of your attacker with the other. (Illustration 5x) If both feet are captured, draw them both in, pulling your assailant off balance, and then "launch" him by forcefully straightening out your legs. (See Illustrations 5y - 5z).

Having an attacker on top of you can be an intimidating experience. Being choked while you are on the ground can be dealt with as follows: 1) bring your right knee up sharply, placing your foot flat on the ground for bracing; 2)cross your wrists over your assailant's forearms and bring them down to your chest forcefully, pinning his arms and bringing his face into striking range; 3) jam your fingers into his eyes; 4) cup his chin with your right hand, and with your left hand reach behind his head, grabbing hair (or if it is too short or if there is none, grab an ear), and sharply twist in a counterclockwise manner (the body follows the direction the head is twisted), while using your right foot to push your right hip up and roll you over on top of your assailant. Now you are in a superior position and can use any of your natural weapons (from Chapter Three) on any of his vital targets until you can safely walk away. (See Illustrations 5aa - 5dd). If you wish to roll your assailant the opposite direction, reverse hand and foot positions.

Arms pinned can be handled in the following manner: Victim face up — 1) plant right foot flat on the ground, bring knee up between assailants legs; 2) slide right hand to meet left hand (doing this changes the weight distribution of your assailant, making him an easily unbalanced "tripod"); 3) push with right foot to raise right hip and roll towards the left. Now finish with attack on vital targets as suggested with previous maneuver. (See Illustrations 5ee -5gg). Victim face down — 1) pull right arm across your chest; 2) lay your head and shoulder hard against assailant's right upper arm; 3) push with left foot and roll assailant off of your left side, pinning his right arm. Now use your feet, elbows, head, etc. to finish the job. (See Illustrations 5hh - 5kk). These techniques are useful in attempted rape situations, and can easily be executed by small women and most girls.

These are only a few of the many groundfighting techniques which have been developed and perfected over the years by self-defense experts. Many of these techniques, such as ones for multiple or armed attackers, or redirecting front or side "dives", for example, are best taught in a "hands-on" environment by professionals who can assure safety for the students with proper supervision, appropriate padding for "the attackers", and crash (landing) pads for all, to soften the falls during practice. A book is not the place to learn some of these techniques, so no attempt to describe them will be made here.

It should be noted that falling to the ground, whether voluntarily or involuntarily, without suffering any injuries, takes some "know-how". You must take care to keep your chin tucked in firmly *so you do not strike the back of your head on the ground.* It is better to bend your knees and fall back on your buttocks than to try to break your fall with outstretched arms, *which can cause broken wrists.* However you get there, you must immediately roll into proper groundfighting position. Refer to the section on Sources for Further Training or Information for instructors in your area.

It should be pointed out that the courts have tended to agree that if an attacker continues his aggression toward a victim on the ground, there is usually greater latitude granted for the victim's use of deadly or dangerous force. This is due, in part, to the fact that the body cannot recoil from blows while on the ground, and instead absorbs the shock more fully than when free-standing.

ILLUS. 5R

Proper ground fighting position

ILLUS. 5S

Groundfighting position effective for even small person or child

ILLUS. 5T

Various targets available from this position

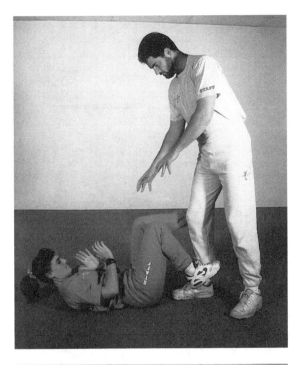

Demonstration of
"Scissor-throw"

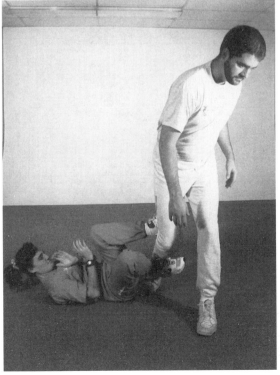

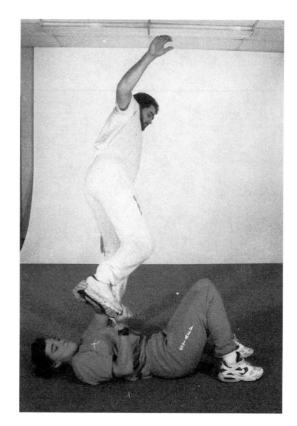

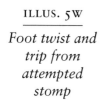

ILLUS. 5W

Foot twist and trip from attempted stomp

ILLUS. 5X

Opposite leg defense if one foot is captured

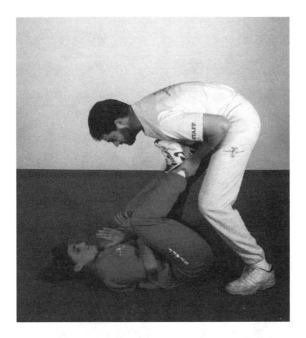

Draw legs up, pulling attacker in to you, and off

Demonstration of defense if both feet are captured

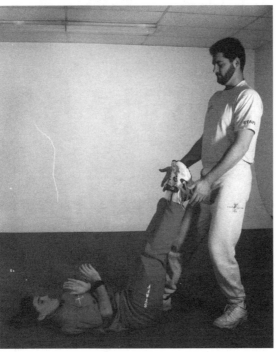

Shoot both legs straight out, knocking attacker down, and away from you

Progression of defensive response to prone choke

ILLUS. 5AA

---

1 of 4

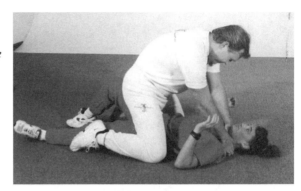

ILLUS. 5BB

---

2 of 4

ILLUS. 5CC

---

3 of 4

ILLUS. 5DD

---

4 of 4

ILLUS. 5EE

1 of 3

Both arms pinned from above

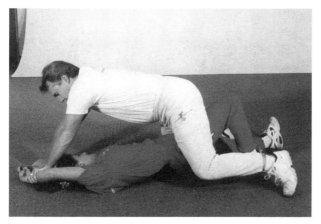

ILLUS. 5FF

2 of 3

Slide both arms to one side, rasie opposite knee, plant foot

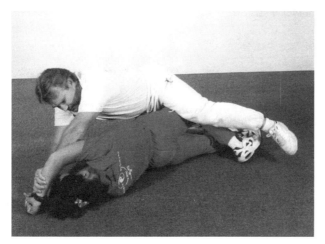

ILLUS. 5GG

3 of 3

Lift hip, push with foot, roll assailant off

ILLUS. 5HH

1 *of* 4

*Face down,
arms pinned*

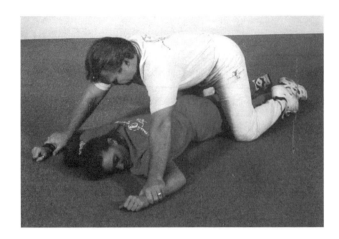

ILLUS. 5II

2 *of* 4

*Pull his arm
tightly under
your chin*

ILLUS. 5JJ

3 *of* 4

*Lean your head
and shoulder
hard against
assailants arm,
push with
opposite leg
and roll him
off*

ILLUS. 5KK

4 of 4

Finish with
elbow strike to
exposed target
area

CHAPTER SIX

MEN'S CONFRONTATIONAL SITUATIONS

*H*istorically, men are fighters. Through the ages, society has tried to "tame" the male animal and turn him into a negotiator rather than a fighter, however, some instincts die hard. When challenged, particularly by another man, most men still lean towards a physical confrontation to prove superiority of the "species". Unfortunately, most of todays threats are of an illegitimate, unexpected nature and may be accompanied by weapons or multiple assailants. Today's confrontations can cost you far more than your honor or your property. Your *life* could be at stake.

Men are more likely than women to be victims of robberies, carjackings, aggravated assaults, assailants armed with weapons and they are more likely to face multiple attacker situations. Men are, by far, the most common murder victims. There are many theories of course, but perhaps the level of violence for men is so pronounced because the assailant believes his risk for injury is greater when he assaults or threatens a man. As a result there is a greater likelihood that more force will be used against a victim that the attacker perceives might harm him, and therefore he comes prepared for resistance. The bottom line is, men are at greater risk for violent assaults, with teenage and young adult males (ages 20–34 years) showing the highest victimization rates.

Just as there are ways that women and children can reduce the risk of being crime victims, men can also take certain precautions. For example, most men carry a wallet (with all their money, identification and credit cards) very predictably in one of two places: If they are wearing casual clothes it is in their right rear pocket (unless they are left-handed), and if they are wearing a suit it is in their left inside breast pocket. No mystery here. The bulge is usually noticeable to those who are looking for it, and its presence makes you a target for both pickpockets and robbers. The simplest way to lower the odds that you will be attacked for the contents of your wallet is to: 1) reduce its size by removing and leaving at home all those credit cards you will not need each day and eliminate all but the most essential pieces of identification, such as your drivers license. (This also reduces the resulting problems if you should still lose your wallet in any manner.) 2) moving the wallet or cash and ID to a front pants pocket where it is not so easily distinguished and reached, and where you have more control over it. A visible money belt or fanny pack, while more secure and safer from pickpockets, literally *screams* "valuables inside", and puts you at greater risk for a robbery.

Another way that many businessmen (and women) place themselves in jeopardy is by carrying a briefcase. Sometimes it cannot be helped, however. Care should be taken to avoid carrying cash or negotiable instruments, identification documents, wallet, keys or other valuables such as calculators, computers, recorders, etc. inside the case. If you must transport such items, pretend you are carrying a large neon sign, flashing the words **"The contents of this briefcase can be turned into money for drugs!"**, and walk with a friend, in well-lit areas, paying special attention to your surroundings. Better yet, do everything you can to keep from carrying it.

Most "highway robberies" of individuals and assaults with armed offenders take place at night, between 6:00 P.M. and midnight, according to the Bureau of Justice Statistics. (The Crime of Robbery will be dealt with in depth in Chapter Eight.)

Carjackings, a particularly violent form of robbery, are increasing in numbers across the country. According to the FBI, there is a homicide in approximately 1 out of every 500 robberies, but there are _50_ homicides per 500 carjackings — making it a much more violent and deadly crime. The National Crime Victimization Survey states that an average of 35,000 completed and attempted carjackings took place each year in the United States between 1987 and 1992. In 52% of the carjackings the offender succeeded in stealing the victim's motor vehicle.

Men are three times more likely than women, and blacks were twice as likely as whites to be victimized by carjackers. Persons 35 years of age or older were less likely than younger individuals to become carjacking victims. (Obviously black men under the age of 35 are at the greatest risk, based on current statistics.) Victims were injured in 24% of the completed carjackings and 18% of attempted carjackings in the cases studied. Offenders used a weapon in 77% of all attempted and completed carjackings. Handguns were the most common weapon used in the completed offenses. Offenders were armed with handguns in 60% of completed carjackings and in 17% of attempted carjackings.

Carjackings were more likely to occur in the evening or at night. About two-thirds of all carjackings occurred after dark. Fifty-eight percent of carjackings that occurred at night and 45% of those during the day were completed. Most carjackings occurred away from the victim's home. Twenty-nine percent took place in a parking lot or garage, and 45% occurred in an open area, such as on the street. Eighteen percent occurred at or near the victim's home.

Approximately 62% of all carjacking offenders are between the ages of 18 and 29. Victims identified the offender's race as white in 32% of all carjackings, black in 49%, and Asian or American Indian in 6%. Men committed 87% of all carjackings. Six percent were committed by males and females together. Only 1% of all carjackings were committed by women alone.

Perhaps most surprising was the median value of automobiles stolen in carjackings, which was only $4,000. Forty-six percent were valued at over $5,000; 13% at $2,500 – $4,999; and 41% at $2,499 or less. It is important to realize that there are many different possible motives behind the perpetration of this crime. The less valuable cars are often just as "useful" to the carjackers as the more expensive ones. Some vehicles are obviously stolen for their parts or are to be shipped out of the country for resale on the black market. Others are stolen for the purpose of using them in another crime — for example a robbery or a drive-by shooting (the perpetrators do not want to use their own vehicle and have it identified, tying them to the crime). Or perhaps the car is used for joyriding purposes, possibly to be abandoned, sometimes in salvageable condition, when it runs out of gas!

Frighteningly enough, one of the most common reasons given for the commission of this crime was "just for the hell of it", because the young perpetrators "got a 'rush'" and a "feeling of power" when they forced someone to give up their means of transportation, which, even if it is a piece of junk, is your key to mobility, independence, and income. Without it you probably cannot get to and from work, to the grocery store, take the kids to school, etc. Without it you are *stranded.*

About half (54%) of all completed or attempted carjackings were committed by groups of two or more offenders. Forty-one percent were committed by lone offenders. Suburbanites were less likely than residents of a central city and more likely than rural residents to be victims of a carjacking. (See Diagrams 6–1, 2 and 3)

Since 45% of the carjackings occurred in an open area, such as a street, certain precautions should be taken when driving, both during the day and night. Keep your car doors locked, and your windows rolled up far enough that a hand cannot reach inside. Be vigilant when you must stop for traffic control signals, stop signs, or slow traffic. Leave at least half to a full car's length between your vehicle and the car in front of you when you come to a stop. If you slide right up to that bumper, remember someone else is right up against <u>your</u> rear bumper, boxing you in. If someone ran up to your car and attempted to get in or assault you, then you have nowhere to go. (Yes, this *does* happen in rush hour traffic.) If you left yourself some room, you can probably escape from an assailant, even if you have to cross the double line on the inside lane, or drive over someone's petunias after jumping the curb on the outside lane.

If you observe what appears to be a person, animal or object lying in the street or roadway, drive around them if you can, but <u>*do not stop or slow significantly*</u>. If you cannot avoid them due to other traffic or road conditions, that's too bad for them. You are not at fault. The odds that someone just happened to collapse in the street are extremely small, and it is a commonly used ploy to get you to stop and then rob you. Similarly, beware of anyone who tries to flag you down, appearing to have car trouble or other emergencies along the side of the road. <u>Of course</u> their vehicle

Diagram 6–1

The offender carried a handgun in 60% of completed carjackings, 1987–92

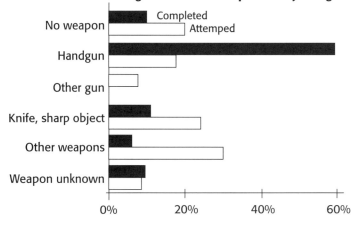

Diagram 6–2

Carjacking compared to risks of other life events

Events	Rate per 1,000 adults per year
Violent victimization	31
Assault (aggravated and simple)	26
Injury in motor vehicle accident	22
Victimization with injury	11
Serious (aggravated) assault	8
Robbery	6
Heart desease death	5
Rape (women only)	1
Motor vehicle accident death	.2
Carjacking	.2
Homicide/legal intervention	.1

Diagram 6–3

53% of completed carjackings were committed by offenders in their 20's

Perceived age of carjacker

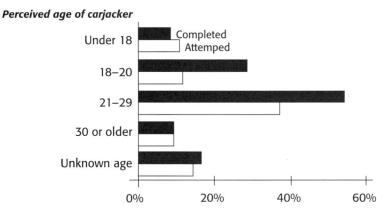

Source: Highlights from 20 Years of Surveying Crime Victims,
October 1993, NCJ-144525.

looks disabled, *they're planning on driving yours!* Often the smallest, most helpless-looking perpetrator will be the decoy. If you feel guilty about passing up a body or a "family" with a broken-down car, go to the nearest *safe* phone and call the police or dial 911 or *55 for the Highway Patrol on your cellular car phone. Unfortunately, many good Samaritans are being victimized when they stop to help a stranger.

If, in spite of all your precautions, you are the victim of a robbery, remember that only your *life* is worth fighting for, your *property* can be replaced. Especially if the perpetrator is armed, or if there are multiple attackers, it is usually best to give them what they want, and hope they take it and go away, leaving you unharmed. If it is *you* that they want, however, then you must fight. (Refer to Suggested Actions to Prevent or Survive a Robbery in Chapter Eight.)

Sometimes men find themselves in physical confrontations when they least expect it. For example, it is not unusual for a simple "fender bender" car accident to suddenly progress from a shouting and pointing match to a shoving and pushing situation, and before you know it a punch has been thrown. Remember that once someone shoves or pushes you, an assault has occurred and it needs to be stopped right there. (In some states, just the slightest touching, such as a finger in your face or chest, constitutes an assault.) Just because this jerk is bigger than you doesn't mean that you have to let him kick sand in your face. Bullies rarely pick on someone their own size, and they usually run home, crying to "mama" when they think they are going to get hurt. Once you open your mouth and threaten them, however, you had better be prepared to put up or shut up!

Men not only have different confrontational situations than women, but different strengths and weaknesses as well. In addition to the natural weapons and vital targets discussed and demonstrated in Chapter Three, the following techniques may be useful in a physical confrontation.

Start by adopting a "safe stance". By this we mean presenting only a side view or an angle to your "possible" antagonist, rather than facing him squarely. This reduces the number of "targets" he can quickly reach, and protects your vital areas. Keep both feet firmly on the ground, spaced comfortably for good balance. Don't place your hands in your pockets or clasp them behind your back. You may need them to quickly block a strike.

How do you know when an individual may be going to assault you? By watching for "pre-attack cues". These include sudden <u>visible sweating</u>, <u>fist clinching</u>, <u>tucking of the chin</u> and <u>rolling of the shoulders</u>, <u>weight shifting</u>, and <u>short-distance pacing</u>. Additional signs to be wary of are <u>repeated phrases</u> (for example: "Do it!", "Do it!", "Do it!", or "You'll be sorry!", "You'll be sorry!", etc.). This often indicates they have lost the ability to think clearly and may act on instinct. <u>Target glancing</u> is another cue which involves pre-occupation with a particular victim or checking out specific targets on a potential victim's body - i.e., looking you over for vulnerabilities. A ploy used for "surprise" attacks is call <u>reaction hand distraction</u>. This is when they use their non-"business" hand to distract your attention, perhaps pointing to something or even lightly punching someone else, then "pow"! They suddenly sucker-punch you when you weren't expecting it. This is a coward's way to fight, since it doesn't give you an opportunity to protect yourself or fight back.

If someone attempts to strike you, you may legally react to protect yourself. Blocking an empty hand assault, which leads to a take down can be accomplished in several ways. Two of our favorites are as follows: 1) Blocking right handed punch with right hand, grasping wrist, extending arm, and using left hand on elbow to execute an arm bar. This can be used to take assailant to the ground and hold him there for an indefinite amount of time. If he gets rowdy, he may receive a broken arm — the one he punches with. (See Illustrations 6a and 6b.); 2) Blocking right handed punch with left hand, gripping wrist and "loading" assailant on your right shoulder as you pull down and forward, rolling or throwing subject on his back at your feet. (See Illustrations 6c - 6f). Use caution if you practice these maneuvers with a *friend*, and use proper padding and crash mats. These techniques do not require a lot of strength. Many women are also able to use these moves. These activities can be reversed and done *left* handed, if your assailant strikes with his left hand, but will probably feel awkward at first if you are right handed.

Wrist locks work well from an attempted front choke or from clothes grabs. With your right hand, reach from underneath and grasp the palm of your assailant, placing your little finger just above his wrist bone. Begin to twist his hand in a clockwise manner while *at the same time* bending it back towards him at the wrist, continuing to apply pressure in both directions until subject is on the ground. (See Illustration 6g and 6h)

Hip throws are a good way to end a grappling match, or at least get your attacker on the ground. From a grappling position, step to the left and place your hip firmly *behind and against his*, keeping your weight and balance *forward*. Now use your right arm and upper body to throw your assailant in a downward arc, backwards around your hip. (Illustrations 6i - 6k).

Anyone who has ever watched a football game knows how effective a good waist tackle can be, and you don't have to be a big guy to knock someone off their feet with it. It has the additional advantage of possibly knocking the breath out of them at the same time. The mistake most people make is not tackling low enough, *so get down there and go for it!* (See Illustration 6l) Now when you are both down there on the ground, and you are on top, remember your natural weapons and vital targets.

Naturally, these are only a few of the simpler self defense moves, however these are probably used more than most, and can be easily learned. While all self defense moves, particularly the more elaborate and complicated ones are best taught by professional self defense instructors under controlled circumstances, for those individuals for whom such endeavors are not feasible or readily available in their area, the above possibilities offer a measure of protection in emergency situations. Additional moves useful in armed and multiple attacker situations, suitable for use by both men and women, follow in Chapter Seven.

ILLUS. 6A

1 of 2

Blocking punch and grasping wrist

How to convert an empty hand assault attempt into an "armbar"

ILLUS. 6B

2 of 2

Pull arm straight, apply pressure to outside of elbow

ILLUS. 6C

1 of 4

Converting empty hand assault into shoulder throw (con't on next page)

ILLUS. 6D

2 of 4

Converting empty hand assault into shoulder throw (con't from previous page)

ILLUS. 6G

---

1 of 2

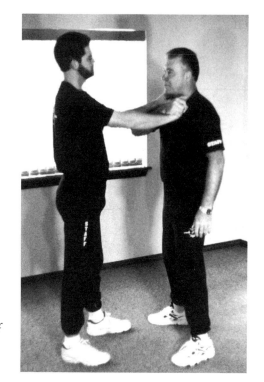

Demonstration of "wrist lock" technique from clothes grab or choke assault

ILLUS. 6H

---

2 of 2

ILLUS. 6I

1 of 3

ILLUS. 6J

2 of 3

Demonstration of a "hip throw"

ILLUS. 6K

3 of 3

ILLUS. 6L

Demonstration of
"waist tackle"

CHAPTER SEVEN

DEALING WITH ARMED AND MULTIPLE ASSAILANTS

With the exception of rape, most violent crimes are very likely to be committed with a weapon of some sort. Firearms are, of course, the most common weapon of choice, being used in almost 70% of all murders and 41% of the robberies, according to the most recent figures available from the Department of Justice. Approximately 17% of the murders, and 15% of the robberies, however, involve the use of a knife or other weapon. As a result, the odds are in favor of a weapon being present if you are the victim of a violent crime. It is, therefore, important to know how to best protect yourself from these weapons, if your life, or that of someone you care about, is at stake.

Warning: The following suggestions for physically confronting armed or multiple attackers are _only_ to be implemented if you believe your life is in imminent jeopardy. These techniques should be practiced to determine your level of competency and capability _before_ your life depends on their proper execution. _Never_ practice with a real gun (even if it is unloaded) or knife. Plastic water pistols and soft toy rubber knives are "real" enough to train with. (If you get wet using a water pistol to execute these moves — _keep practicing_, you're doing something wrong!)

Most attackers armed with a gun will approach you when you are alone and will show the weapon to you, or _poke_ you with it. As a matter of fact, they usually _want_ you to see that they really have it and be frightened enough of it to do what they tell you to do. Robberies with a firearm are usually very "up close and personal", with the gunman very close to you, often poking you with the barrel of the gun. Now, believe it or not, this is to your advantage. If the attacker is several feet away and is seriously threatening you, you are too far away (unless you are _very_ good and _very_ fast) to attempt to take control of the weapon. Up close, it is pretty simple to perform disarming techniques.

Before you decide you must grab for the gun, however, consider your circumstances and the actual risk to you. If you are where you can probably be seen and heard by others, for example in a parking lot or public garage, it is possible that the gunman has no intention of actually *firing* the weapon. He is most likely using it to intimidate you and insure your compliance. If he *shoots* the firearm, it will attract attention, something he doesn't want because someone will undoubtedly hear and possibly be able to identify him. There are, of course, no guarantees about the behavior of a violent criminal. Review the "red flag situations" outlined in Chapter Eight in the section dealing with Robbery Prevention for more definitive information on *when* to resist or take defensive actions.

If you believe that the gunman *does* intend to kill you, then you must take control of the weapon. It helps to know if the weapon pointed at you is a revolver or a semi-automatic. Semi-automatics seem to be more and more prevalent as street weapons these days. One thing you know for certain, however, is that you cannot be shot if the weapon is not pointing at you! Therefore, the first thing you must do is get that sucker pointed away from you. This can be accomplished in the following manner if the shooter is standing in front of you, and holding the weapon in his right hand. First, go *Hollywood!* Raise your hands just like you have seen it done in hundreds of "stick-ups" in the movies, and stare at the gun. Then, since that tends to attract attention in a parking lot and *everyone* knows what it means, the assailant will tell you to "Put your hands down!", which gives you permission to move. When you do so, quickly bring your *left* hand down over the barrel of an automatic or over the cylinder of a revolver, grasping it tightly and redirecting it away from your body. (See Illustrations 7a and 7b) If the gun is a fully loaded and chambered semi-automatic, one round can go off at this time. If, however, you are gripping the barrel (which *will* become hot, but not unbearably so), you have prevented the automatic reloading function and caused the weapon to jam. If the gun is a revolver and you are gripping the cylinder, preventing it from turning, it cannot fire until you release it. Practice this with a water pistol, with your "assailant" attempting to fire as soon as you grab for the gun. (Remember that a *real* assailant will not be expecting you to do this, and will be taken by surprise. By the time he tries to pull the trigger, the gun should be pointing well away from your body.)

The second part of this maneuver is as follows. Bring your right hand up under the barrel of the weapon and drive it into your assailant's face, continuing to force it down his chest and stomach, until he either lets go of the weapon, shoots himself, or his finger breaks in the trigger guard, giving you final control of the weapon. (See Illustration 7c) Most firearms have front sights on the topside of the barrel, which are usually fairly sharp and serrated. These will definitely "smart" as they are scraped across bare or thinly covered skin. Now practice this technique *left-handed,* since there is about a 15% chance that your attacker will be a "southpaw".

What if the gunman is not in front of you? As long as you can feel and/or see a firearm within easy reach from a "hands-up" position, you can take control of it and redirect it away from your body. See Illustrations 7d - 7h for examples of how this can be done. Again, practice is important to build skill, speed and confidence. You are not as likely to use a technique you have never tried as you are to attempt one you have rehearsed, especially in an emergency situation.

There are a number of other techniques for disarming an individual with a firearm, but they require a slightly higher level of expertise and should be taught in a "hands on" environment. Similarly, there are a number of techniques designed to defeat disarming attempts, should someone grab *your* gun, however, it is inappropriate to try to teach them in a book. For knowledgeable defensive firearms instructors in your area, refer to the section of this book on Sources for Further Training or Information.

Defending against an attacker armed with a knife is a risky business. Never be the one to introduce a knife into a fight, because the risk of everyone getting cut is very high. Knife wounds are nasty and often deadlier than bullet wounds. (See Diagram 3-2 on Page 49). The primary self-defense principle to remember when dealing with a knife-wielding attacker is two-fold: *control and redirect.* In the type of attack shown in Illustration 7i and 7j, one must catch and secure the wrist of the assailant as demonstrated, then as part of the same fluid movement, redirect his arm across his body and apply pressure with your elbow and upper arm to the back of his elbow, bringing him down (or breaking his arm) as the situation dictates. As you apply pressure to his arm, you can "wring" his wrist, (remember the "Indian rope burns" of your childhood days?), demanding that he drop the knife to avoid further pain and/or injuries. When he drops the knife, kick it well out of reach.

In the scenario depicted in Illustration 7k - 7m, the knife hand must again be captured and secured as shown. Then, with the wrist firmly grasped, quickly turn and bring the attacker's arm down sharply across your shoulder, which will probably break or dislocate it.

Being outnumbered in a violent confrontation is always dangerous. In addition to the Pre-Attack Cues we listed in Chapter Six, there are some additional cues to be aware of when there are multiple attackers. These include: movement in relationship to each other (they have done this before and are now assuming their "normal" fight positions or pecking order); glancing at each other for readiness cues; secondary opponent distraction (they fake a situation with each other or a non-target victim to get close to and surprise the *real* target — much like the *reaction hand distraction* ploy discussed in Chapter Six); and finally, code or hand signals (popular with gang members). Noticing these cues can allow you to take proper self-defense actions.

Making the *first move* toward combat engagement *and* being the one who *chooses which assailant to fight* are usually the keys to survival in a multiple attacker situation. If you allow yourself to be surrounded and wait until your assailants execute *their* plan, you will probably have to fight each and every one of them, either all at once or in ascending order of size, strength and leadership within their gang. This usually means the toughest and most powerful, or the ringleader of the group, will be taking you on *after* you have little or no more strength left to fight him. He will then usually have the "honor" of finishing you off, after some "macho posturing", which insures his dominance with the rest of the gang.

There are a couple of ways to thwart their plan and, while there are never any guarantees when you are surprised and outnumbered, your odds of survival can be substantially increased. The first and best option, if possible, after determining that a fight is inevitable, would be to identify the leader and initiate combat with him while you are at your strongest. If you defeat him, you *may* not have to fight the rest, for two reasons. There is a definite "pecking order" in nearly any gang, with the one who has the reputation for being the toughest and meanest normally being the leader. If his followers see him defeated or injured by someone, they tend to be disinclined to put themselves at risk for the same punishment by that person. (Gang members are like packs of dogs — rarely are they very brave as individuals.) Secondly, it is often considered inappropriate to "shame" their leader by winning a fight he has lost. There is a real chance that they will drag their injured leader off and leave you alone. Even if you have to continue to fight, you now have a significant psychological advantage, and you will be fighting individuals with *decreasing* strength and skill. If, however, this individual is at the *center* of the gang approaching you, this is probably not a good tactical choice, since his buddies will surround and overwhelm you. See Illustration 7n.

The second option is to select an assailant on either end of the approaching gang. As you initiate combat with this individual, place him strategically between you and the other assailants, using him as a shield. If he falls, he will most likely take another attacker down with him. See Illustration 7o.

In addition to causing an assailant to fall backwards and create a "domino" effect, there are several other simple ways to take out more than one attacker at a time. For example, see how the arm bars discussed in Chapter Six can be used to *direct* one assailant into another, as shown in Illustration 7p - 7q. Similarly, the shoulder throw shown in Illustrations 6c - 6f is effective in a multiple attacker situation, when the attacker is thrown against the other assailants.

Another approach for a moderately athletic individual is to aim your right shoulder in a rolling dive at the left shin of an outside attacker, trapping his ankle and placing your weight on his instep. As you continue your roll against that attacker, causing him to fall and break his ankle because you are pinning his foot to the ground, extend and swing your left leg solidly into the groin of the attacker adjacent to the first. Now, if you must continue to fight, you can readily assume a groundfighting position, as discussed in Chapter Five. This position has advantages for men as well as for women. (See Illustrations 7r - 7t). When practicing this move, use extreme caution not to actually pin the foot of your practice partner, because injuries are almost inevitable. This is best practiced using only inanimate "dummies".

Another effective maneuver when attacked by multiple assailants is executed from a grappling position, such as a "clothes grab" or frontal choke. Firmly grasp and pin the left wrist of the attacker with your left hand, then bring your right hand up and over your attackers arm into a roundhouse palm strike to the jaw, and, *with no break of momentum*, continue with a finger jab into the eyes of the second attacker who is standing to the right of the initial assailant. This action is likely to break the wrist of the first attacker, effectively giving you the advantage over two injured opponents. See Illustrations 7u - 7w. As with all of the self-defense techniques presented, these may be reversed or executed "left-handed", and should be practiced both ways.

Also very important in any mutual combat situation, never let them make you back up or walk backwards. The body is not designed to move effeciently in a backwards direction, so not only can you not move efficiently or swiftly in that direction, but you are off balance, cannot see where you are going, and are, therefore, more likely to fall or trip, particularly when you are under unusual stress. Likewise, your attackers cannot move backwards efficiently either, so it is to your advantage to force them to do just that. As we mentioned in Chapter Five when discussing groundfighting, one must take care if they *do* start to fall backwards, to tuck their chin and avoid hitting the back of their head, even on a carpeted or "soft" floor.

We are presupposing that no lethal weapons are present in the confrontations outlined above. Weapons pose a major additional threat to survival and additional or alternate strategies may be needed.

ILLUS. 7A

1 of 3

Going "Hollywood" during a "stick-up"

ILLUS. 7B

2 of 3

Grabbing and straight-arming the barrel of the gun, pointing away from you

Illus. 7C

3 of 3

*Grabbing barrel
with other hand
and pointing it
towards assailant*

Disarming armed assailant (rear assault)

ILLUS. 7F

3 of 3

ILLUS. 7G

1 of 2

Disarming armed assailant (side assault)

ILLUS. 7H

2 of 2

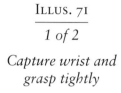

ILLUS. 7I

1 of 2

Capture wrist and grasp tightly

Knife assault defense (from downward strike)

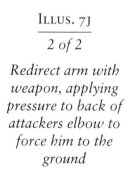

ILLUS. 7J

2 of 2

Redirect arm with weapon, applying pressure to back of attackers elbow to force him to the ground

ILLUS. 7K

1 of 3

Capture upthrust knife hand firmly at wrist

Knife assault defense (from upward strike)

ILLUS. 7L

2 of 3

If grasping attackers right wrist, turn to the right and bring arm over left shoulder

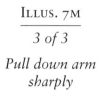

ILLUS. 7M

3 of 3

*Pull down arm
sharply*

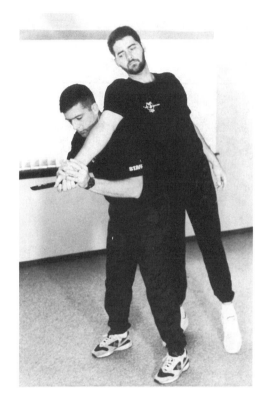

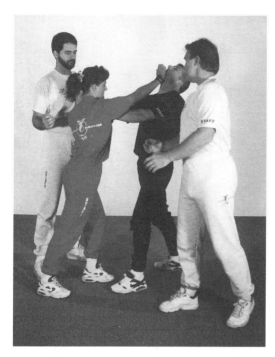

ILLUS. 7N

Improper *choice of central assailant, allowing encirclement of victim*

Initiating engagement of multiple attackers

ILLUS. 7O

Choosing an assailant at either end provides some protection

*Demonstration
of "block and
armbar" used to
combat two
assailants*

ILLUS. 7R

1 of 3

Charge the leg of one attacker

Effectively disabling two attackers at once

ILLUS. 7S

2 of 3

Trap his ankle and place weight on foot, rolling against his shin

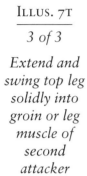

ILLUS. 7T

3 of 3

Extend and swing top leg solidly into groin or leg muscle of second attacker

ILLUS. 7U

1 of 3

Grasp outside wrist and pin to shoulder

Effectively disabling two attackers at once from "clothes grab" or choke

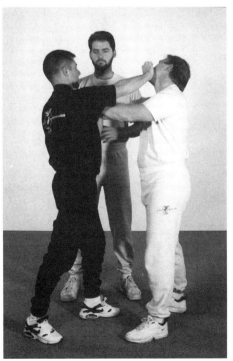

ILLUS. 7V

2 of 3

Cross over with strike to jaw

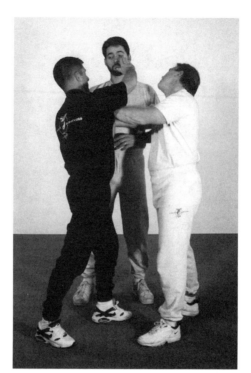

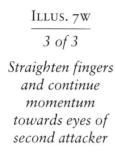

Straighten fingers and continue momentum towards eyes of second attacker

CHAPTER EIGHT

WORKPLACE VIOLENCE — CAUSES AND CURES

*M*ost of us think that our workplace is safe, and that the dangers and hostile behavior we may encounter elsewhere do not exist or are very rare at our place of employment. The reality is that violence in America is spilling out of the streets and into the workplace. A recent Justice Department Report states that one-sixth of all violent crimes occur at work. The workplace is the scene of almost two million violent crimes every year, according to a 1993 survey by Northwestern National Life Insurance Company. It is estimated that at least 10% of these crimes involve offenders armed with handguns.

In 1995, the U.S. Department of Labor reported *homicide was, once again, the 2nd leading cause of death at work*, surpassing fires, falls and electrocutions. Work related vehicular accidents were only slightly higher, at number one. Approximately 26 people a week are now killed in the workplace. In addition, during the past year, one out of four American workers was attacked, threatened or harassed on the job. More than two million Americans were attacked at work, over 6.3 million were threatened, and 16.1 million were harassed. Those statistics include incidents of violence where the victim knew, *and did not know*, the attacker. An estimated 8 percent of all rapes, 7 percent of all robberies, 16 percent of all assaults, and more than 5 percent of all homicides occur at work. At the same time, 2 million personal thefts and more than 200,000 car thefts occur each year while people are at work, as reported by the National Criminal Victimization Survey.

In the Northwestern study, 15 percent of the workers surveyed said they had been physically attacked on the job at some time during their working life, and 21 percent said they had been threatened with physical harm. One in six (18%) of the attacks on the job was with a lethal weapon. Actual physical attacks were *twice* as likely to be from a customer, client or patient than from a co-worker or stranger. A Northeastern University Sociology and Criminol-

ogy Professor has been quoted, however, as stating that recent figures show the number of *bosses* killed at work has *doubled* over
the past 10 years, with three to four a month slain by a disgruntled
worker or ex-worker.

Although such acts can happen at any business, the majority
tend to occur in the service sector, where employees are working
for minimum wage and the lowest job skills are required. Approximately half of all workplace homicide victims were workers in
retail establishments. Fourteen percent of all violent crimes occur
when the victim is "on duty". Women and teens figure disproportionately in this category, with women at a significantly higher risk
than men. *Fifty percent of women who die at work do so at the
hands of a murderer* — with men it is only about ten percent, even
though three times as many males were murdered at work. Other
worker categories with an unusually high proportion of fatalities
due to homicide include the self-employed, workers 16 and 17
years old, Hispanics and non-whites, except American Indians.

Robbery was the primary motive for nearly 71% of the homicides at work, according to the Labor Department. Four percent
were victims of current or former spouses, lovers or other relative.
Most of the homicide victims were shot (75%); 7 percent were
stabbed; 13 percent were killed by bombs or fires; the others were
beaten, strangled, or purposely run over by a vehicle. (Due to the
enormous loss of lives in the April 19, 1995 bombing of the Federal
Building in Oklahoma City, the percentage of those killed by
bombs may be higher than usual, however bombings are, unfortunately, becoming much more common.) The highest percentage of
workplace homicides occur in or around buildings or businesses
open to the public, parking lots, garages, and apartment buildings.

Half the victims of workplace homicide worked in either a sales
occupation (such as sales clerk, retail store owner, or cashier) or a
service related occupation (such as police officer, security guard, or
food preparer). Taxicab drivers and various management-related
occupations also reported high numbers of job related homicides.
The retail trade accounted for 41 percent of all workplace homicides in 1995. Homicides in convenience and other grocery stores,
eating and drinking places, and gasoline service stations predomi-

nated among retail establishments. Government workers accounted for one-fifth of the homicide victims, twice as many as the previous year because of the Oklahoma City bombing.

Workers in healthcare, community services, and retail settings
suffer the greatest number of *nonfatal assaults.* (25% of all
patients in the E.R. are carrying a weapon, and more than 17% of
all mental patients are armed when first brought to a hospital or
healthcare facility.)

The top three most dangerous occupations (with the highest
number of fatalities in the most recent annual report by the Department of Labor) were, in order:

1) Supervisors, proprietors, sales occupations (63% of these
   deaths at work were homicides);

2) Police and detectives (public, not private security), (47%
   of these workplace deaths were homicides);

3) Cashiers (92% of all cashiers who died at work were
   homicide victims). Taxicab drivers were listed next and
   continue to be one of the most dangerous professions.

It should be noted that the increases in the number of fatalities
would be far greater if customers, children, passersby and other
non- or off-duty employees who are also killed during these violent
rampages were included in the figures. The Department of Labor
only counts "on-duty employees" in their statistics. For example,
in Oklahoma City, only those victims who were *working* at the
facility at the time of the bomb were counted, _not_ any of those
killed who were there in the daycare center, who were clients or
customers of the various agencies, who worked there but were on
"off-duty time", or who were in the parking lot or passing by, or in
an adjacent building (unless they were "at work" at that location).
The actual, total number of individuals killed each year in workplace homicide incidents is unknown, but could easily be expected
to double or even triple the statistics now given.

Terrorist Threats

A recent FBI report on **terrorism** on U.S. soil prepared by the
National Security Division of the U.S. Department of Justice, lists

approximately 250 incidents of terrorism in the past fifteen years. The report states that "The threat posed by terrorism is transforming and can, at times, intensify in direct relation to changes in political, social, and economic situations occurring around the world." There have been 30 such incidents in the past five years, including the bombing of the Federal Building in Oklahoma City.

Of these 30 terroristic acts, 12 were conducted by Puerto Rican groups and 13 by special interest groups, two by right-wing interests and one by a left-wing interest. Only two were identified as acts of international terrorism, including the February 26, 1993 bombing of the World Trade enter, which killed six and injured 1,000 people. These 30 terroristic incidents by the way, do <u>not</u> include attacks on abortion clinics, but such attacks may well be included in future reports according to U.S. Attorney General Janet Reno, since 32 abortion clinic-related cases that involved actual acts of violence or threats were investigated by the FBI in 1994 alone. Of the 30 incidents that *were* listed in the report, 23 involved bombing, four were arson. Also included were hijacking, assassination, sabotage, robbery, kidnapping, hostile takeovers and malicious destruction of property.

Fourteen of these attacks occurred at commercial establishments, nine at military establishments, four on state or federal property, and one each at a diplomatic establishment, private home or car, and a school. The report defines a terrorist incident *as a violent act to intimidate or coerce a government, the civilian population or any segment, to further political or social objectives.*

Possible terrorist acts aside, according to the National Institute of Occupational Safety and Health (NIOSH), workplaces which have the highest risk of work-related homicides include:

* Taxicab establishments
* Liquor stores
* Gas stations
* Detective/Protective Services
* Grocery stores
* Jewelry stores
* Hotels/motels
* Eating/drinking places

NIOSH further lists the following occupations as the most likely to expose the worker to the threat of workplace homicide:

* Taxicab drivers/chauffeurs
* Law enforcement officers (police officers/sheriffs)
* Hotel clerks
* Gas station workers
* Security guards
* Stock handlers/baggers
* Store owners/managers
* Bartenders

The factors that may *increase* the risk of homicide are:

* Exchange of money with the public
* Working alone or in small numbers
* Working late night or early morning hours
* Working in high-crime areas
* Guarding valuable property or possessions
* Working in community settings

Employers Guide to a Safe Workplace

While reports of violent acts in the workplace have been increasingly common during the past few years, only recently have many employers gotten serious about doing anything about it. Not only are they trying to protect their employees and customers, but they are recognizing the tremendous legal liabilities they may face if they do not address safety and security issues *before* a violent incident occurs. Random acts of violence are impossible to predict accurately, but one *can* develop an awareness of the *likelihood* of such an act, identify and remedy weak areas of security, and take steps to cut down on the risk of employees who might cause problems.

Pre-employment screening is one option. Some employers object to the cost of background checks, and of course, you can't always get information on mental health records. There are, however, several nationwide companies that can check out criminal history and other types of background information for as little as

$25.00. Obviously, simply having a criminal history does not mean a worker will turn violent, however the court rulings tend to suggest that an employer ought to make an effort to uncover past criminal history. Employers can be found guilty of "negligent hiring" if an employee with a criminal background goes on to commit another crime at the workplace. Some states have introduced legislation that would make it easier to check employee backgrounds by shielding employers from liability for giving references.

Legal authorities stress that employers have other obligations beyond checking workers criminal histories. Companies have a duty to protect their employees and customers if there are indications of incipient violence. While the employer has some responsibilities to protect the rights of an employee who, let us say for example, may be acting in a bizarre manner or who may have threatened an act of violence, the employer has a greater duty to those whose lives may be in danger from this individual. The law is not clearly defined here — except if the employer knows his employees or customers may be in danger, he's got a duty to *warn* them of the danger or *protect* them from the danger. Some employers have gone so far as to obtain protective orders on behalf of employees in an effort to protect them against perceived danger.

From a corporate standpoint, goodwill and honest concern for employee and customer safety aside, one important reason for addressing the potential homicide and/or violent attack problem are workmen's compensation issues and "premises' liability" legal concerns. Workmen's compensation costs have skyrocketed throughout the United States in almost every industry. The impact of a mass murder or violent attack on a business has disastrous effects on the cost and availability of Workmen's Compensation Insurance. In addition, premises' liability laws have recently been interpreted to suggest that these laws apply to victims of workplace violence *and families* of victims. Since many courts have abandoned old tort rules requiring plaintiffs to produce evidence of the "foreseeability" of a homicide or other violent incident, this law puts businesses on notice that they had better have a corporate policy and plan directed at containing any and all violence in the workplace. *To ignore the probability of workplace violence would*

not be a judicious decision by management. Therefore, it is necessary to examine various means to prepare for a violent act, including a homicide or multiple homicides, in a company. These strategies may be divided into three basic categories: (I) Company
Policies and Procedures; (II) Employee Training; and (III) Security
Hardware and Personnel.

I. Company policies.

Corporations can make fundamental changes in policy that can
help stem the rate of homicides and violent incidents at the workplace. These decisions should be made in conjunction with under-
taking a security audit of the entire organization. Frequently
implemented policies include:

a) <u>Reduce exposure to high risk environments.</u> Businesses
can limit their exposure to high crime areas as well as to high
crime time periods, i.e., late night or early morning. Tradi-
tional urban establishments have begun to locate or relocate
in suburban and rural areas. In addition, closing retail outlets to in-store customers and serving through bullet-proof
and/or drive-through windows, or simply adopting a midnight closing time, have become commonly acceptable practices in the fast food and convenience store industries and are
procedures now being adopted by many other retail outlets.

Additional risk factors which should be addressed are 1)
proximity to major highways which provide easy access
and quick get-aways and/or escape routes; and 2) remote
locations which are not located near other open businesses.

b) <u>Forming strategic alliances to combat criminal elements.</u>
Businesses have begun to ban together to address workplace violence. Local crime prevention associations are
being formed that hire off-duty police and provide training
for managers and employees dealing with violent criminals.

c) <u>Increasing the number of employees.</u> Some retail establishments are following the lead of many police departments and are increasing the number of employees during
high crime hours in select locations. The cost of this strate-

gy may seem to be high, given the level of business during high crime hours, but may be one of the only ways to offer safeguards for employees in these potentially high crime situations. One of the "top five attractiveness features" given by convicted robbers for choosing a store to rob was "only one clerk on duty". They also stated that "inattentive" and "female clerks on duty alone" were choice targets.

d) Explore community involvement programs. If a substantial portion of the workplace violence can be attributed to "low self-control" individuals, corporations must aggressively become involved in community programs, according to a recent study by Richard A. Cosier, Dean of the College of Business Administration, University of Oklahoma. These programs should address the development period in the socialization process of children. This type of community involvement would serve two primary purposes: (1) help establish basic behavioral standards for children who are not provided these guidelines in the home, and (2) to represent a visual sign to the local community that the company is making a contribution to the development of youth as well as to the citizenry as a whole, all of which should tend to make the company, and its employees, less desirable targets of neighborhood criminal activity.

e) Formulate Company Policies for Emergency Preparedness. To deal effectively with any and all crisis situations *including* violence, homicides or mass murders in the workplace, companies need a well-articulated emergency preparedness manual. The policies and procedures set forth therein should address the organization member's performance, communications to the public, (i.e. all interested parties both internally and externally) and the overall organizational performance during the incident.

The initial stage in developing such a crisis management program involves the emergency plan itself, formulating emergency management teams, training personnel to respond properly during a crisis, and gathering resources to address a crisis situation. A strategic planning effort is needed to heighten awareness and to insure that a plan exists to deal effectively with the crisis. The management team would ideally be composed of division directors from Personnel, Legal, Safety & Security, and Operations & Maintenance. Representatives from all other divisions would be beneficial. Often, where some type of emergency preparedness manual already exists for natural disasters such as fires, tornadoes or hurricanes, floods, etc., it can be expanded and further implemented to include potential violent incidents.

The second element to be addressed in a strategy to combat homicides in the workplace is training employees to identify and deal with potentially dangerous "low self-control" individuals in the workplace. See Illustration 8a.

II. Employee Training

Due to the difficulty in predicting aggressive criminal behavior in a business environment, employees become one, if not the best, deterrent to violence in the workplace. It is up to employers to encourage workers to report signs indicating a co-worker may have the potential to commit violence at the workplace. Not only must employees be made aware of the problem, they must be given appropriate and sufficient training to respond in a manner that will help not only themselves, but will also be in the best interests of the company, co-workers and the public, in the event of a criminal act. The management team suggested above should be in place to participate actively and guide the resolution of any conflict situation. Studies of workplace violence incidents dating back to the mid-1980's show that many of them involved some sort of workplace conflict, with a high percentage of incidents appearing to be related to the firing of or other disciplinary actions taken against the perpetrator.

Employees who turn violent typically feel helpless and hopeless and see violence as the only solution to their problem. Signs of potential problem behavior include:

* Moodiness, irritability and paranoia
* A negative change in behavior, or possibly suddenly impulsive or withdrawn

  * Sudden tardiness to work, or failure to complete assignments
  * Screaming or swearing episodes at work
  * Excessive absenteeism, abuse of sick and/or personal leave
  * Alcohol or drug use, ignoring company policies

Aberrant behavior can usually be spotted by co-workers and should be reported so that action can be taken to defuse a potentially violent situation. Reporting procedures and chain of command will vary according to employer, but should be clearly outlined in each company's Policies and Procedures Manual, including provisions for skipping chain of command in the event it is a *supervisor* that is the subject of concern.

Several recent studies have concurred that there are three common profiles of people who commit such acts of violence on the job. Some individuals may exhibit characteristics of more than one category.

1) *The Chronic Disgruntled Complainer.* This is usually a male in his 40's who is overly aggressive, a marginal performer, with an exaggerated sense of entitlement and who is difficult to supervise.

2) *The Romantic Obsessive.* This is also usually a male who is focused on an idealized romantic union and believes those feelings are mutual. He exhibits a love/hate relationship toward women with his perception being clouded by denial and self-deception. He cannot handle rejection and will not take "No!" for an answer.

3) *The Domestic Abuser.* This individual is a spouse beater/abuser at home who may bring the violence to the workplace. This often occurs during an estrangement situation, as he/she stalks and harasses the former marital or romantic partner.

There are, of course, individuals who commit violent acts at the workplace who do not fall into one of these three categories, however, these profiles are *one* of the tools we can use to attempt to determine if an individual is likely to become violent. It is always important for both employers and employees to try to identify a potential problem and defuse it before it erupts. More and more we are seeing that what happens outside the workplace can affect what happens in it. Employers need to be more focused on whether the job is a good fit intellectually and emotionally and need to make more of an effort to check the background both personally and professionally of the individuals they hire, and encourage co-workers to notice and report possible problems with an employee *before* the episode becomes physically violent.

Personal problems are not the only catalyst for violence at work. Unfortunately, many times employers concerned about eliminating workplace violence need only to look at their own management, which may be as blameworthy as the violent employee. Experts in this field suggest that in many cases the individual would probably never have resorted to violence if he or she had a manager or supervisor who was compassionate and who took an interest in their employees. Studies have shown that several corporate factors can contribute to the possibility of violence in the workplace. These factors include:

* Autocratic, authoritarian bosses
* Deceitful and manipulative management
* Favoritism, nepotism
* Poor lines of communication between subordinates and superiors and between co-workers themselves
* Unjustified promotions or raises
* Intimidation of subordinates
* Arrogance and paranoia on the part of management
* Insensitive firings, with no attempt at outplacement

During all employee training and orientation sessions, certain specific goals should be accomplished:

a) Achieve a heightened awareness by employees of violent potential in the workplace. Remember, one cannot prepare for what one does not expect to ever happen. Recognition of danger signs *must be reported immediately*. Training programs to address violence and a corporate response to it must permeate all levels in the organization. Top management has to make a conscious decision to address this significant issue. Middle managers have to be able to effectively manage the planning process to deal with a conflict as well as the aftermath of such an attack. *Employees must recognize that their behavior before and during the assault can have a dramatic impact on the outcome of such an attack.*

b) Daily security checklist/procedures. Safety is everyone's responsibility and therefore the entire organization must address security issues daily. Without this discipline from the corporation and input from all levels of the organization, a security program cannot be effective. Every effort should be made to create an environment that is not conducive to adverse behavior by "low self-control" individuals. Examples of such procedures would be regularly checking parking lots for unauthorized vehicles; changing any security codes or locks immediately if there is a termination; immediate notification of front-line people (such as reception and security) if a security risk of any type exists; keeping accurate lists of all individuals who have access to important or restricted corporate documents and/or main frame computer systems. Access to the workplace should be restricted to those who are presently "on duty", and visitors (including off duty employees) should be allowed only with *written* supervisory approval. It is important, for both security *and safety* reasons, to know who is in the building, and why, at any given time. Illustration 8c, Bomb Threat Check List, was designed for operators or receptionists who answer the business phones.

c) Training employees on **hostage** rules. Employees who have been prepared to deal with the possibility of being held hostage are far more likely to survive the ordeal. Their behavior during this time period may determine their fate and the probability of a successful resolution of the crisis. The crisis environment of a workplace homicide resembles the characteristics of a terrorist attack. Employees, there-

fore, must recognize that they are neither heroes nor martyrs
and that they should not take on either of these roles.
Understanding the chronology of a crisis ordeal is essential
to dealing with it effectively, and can prevent victims from
inadvertently compounding the severity of the situation by
improper actions. The objective of this training is to survive
the crisis by recognizing the stages through which it will
progress. According to a recent University of Oklahoma
research paper, these stages are as follows:

(1) <u>Startle/panic</u> — The victim experiences an intense
burst of adrenalin which, without a plan to follow,
may become feelings of fear, defenselessness, confusion, and disorientation, which can then lead to
"frozen fright";

2) <u>Disbelief</u> — Startle and panic normally give way to
denial, which tends to numb the reasoning process of
the hostage. They often assume (unfortunately wrong-
fully) that there will be an immediate rescue or retalia-
tion by authorities who won't let the situation continue;

3) <u>Hypervigilence</u> — The victim becomes wary, attentive
to small details. Acutely vigilant behavior follows the
numbness of the first two stages. In this stage, captives
closely "study" their situation in an attempt to make
some sense out of the ordeal. This can be an exercise
in futility, since many times even long after the event,
no clear reason is found for the actions of many violent
individuals;

4) <u>Resistance/Compliance</u> — Hostages often first attempt
to resist any requests and/or orders of their captor
which typically leads to confrontation. Hostages
should recognize that "stone killers" have no feelings
for them or others and, therefore should not be pro-
voked. Each hostage must make an independent decision regarding their own chances for survival if they
continue to obey the captor's demands. "Trained"
individuals will know what their physical self-protec-

tive options are and act accordingly as opportunities may present themselves. Each situation must be evaluated independently based on the risks present;

5) <u>Depression</u> — Psychologically it is necessary, in order to fully accept captivity, to become depressed. Dealing with this stage of "hopelessness" has to be aggressively addressed by hostages; and

6) <u>Acceptance</u> — This stage brings with it a cognitive realization and acceptance that the situation is real and that, possibly, the hostages cannot resolve the situation without outside help, which may take many hours, days or even longer.

Dealing with the stress of the situation provides the victims of hostage situations with a way to handle the ambiguity of the outcome. Proper responses to robbery situations will be discussed later in this chapter.

III. Security Hardware

Fortifying the place of business is often one of the first reactions of management to the potential risks to employees and customers posed by violent crime. The 1993 outlay for security equipment for use in businesses has been estimated to be in excess of $22 Billion per year, up approximately 16 percent from 1990. The amount spent on private security is in excess of the amount spent on all the nation's police departments. This trend toward extra security measures is particularly true of companies who have interaction with the general public. Unfortunately, many employers do not know how to hire properly trained, experienced private security personnel that are capable of detecting and effectively dealing with the criminal element, particularly if it turns violent. Remember that, as an employer, just as in any other job category, *you get what you pay for.* You cannot expect someone who only makes slightly over minimum wage or even $10.00 or $12.00 per hour to perform the same job as a fully trained, experienced police officer, and to intervene successfully in a violent confrontation. It is often worth the extra money to hire off-duty police, who are usually looking for a way to supplement their meager incomes. Another old adage comes to mind: *Good things aren't cheap, and cheap things aren't good.* Go ahead, splurge. It's your <u>life</u> that may be at stake.

A number of different products have been installed by businesses to reduce the opportunity for crime to take place. The following safety related products have been recommended:

a) **Increased lighting** — Improving a facility's indoor and outdoor lighting is one of the most frequent suggestions made by law enforcement agencies in an effort to reduce crime. Criminals are simply not comfortable in a brightly lit area, since their actions can be easily viewed by others, and, as a result, violent crimes such as robbery, rape, auto theft and aggravated assault are less likely to occur. It is the employer's responsibility to keep such areas as employee and customer parking lots safe, as well as the actual business premises.

b) **Increased visibility in work environment** — Shelving and displays have been lowered by many retailers to permit both employees and customers to see throughout the store, eliminating "pockets" of privacy where criminal acts often occur. Facilities in industrial locations have been modified so that visibility is maximized. (This may also cut down on "unobserved" or "unsubstantiated" injury claims.) Office partitions can be transparent or translucent rather than opaque. Sexual assaults and harassment, threats, assaults and even petty theft will drop substantially if the individuals responsible for such actions are not given private access to the object of their aggression or greed. A more open floorplan will substantially reduce the probability of violence by removing the opportunity for uninterrupted and unobserved privacy.

c) **Surveillance cameras** — These are invaluable to record crimes in progress, for continuous, remote monitoring of high crime areas, and have been used successfully for years in banks, convenience stores, hotels and jewelry stores, etc.

These cameras are now often found in office buildings, factories and warehouses, reception areas and restrooms. Surveillance tapes are frequently crucial evidence, in the prosecution of criminals. Because of that fact, they are now often disabled by criminals prior to or during commission of their crimes. As a result, newer, smaller, high-tech cameras are available which are virtually invisible and cannot be easily dismantled. What looks like a sprinkler head or a lovely lamp or even a pencil sharpener, may actually be a camera recording every move that is made. As criminals become more aware of security measures, they will attempt to defeat them. There are a number of large companies now, however, that specialize in "invisible" security hardware and can help you stay one step ahead of the bad guys.

d) **Signs and silent alarms** — There are two schools of thought regarding whether to inform both customers and employees that the company takes covert surveillance measures such as alarm systems, security personnel, random security checks and hidden cameras. While knowledge of these measures may discourage some petty crimes such as theft or embezzlement, an intimate knowledge of all the security measures may enable the violent criminal to evade or disable them.

e) **Bullet proof glass and clothing, peepholes, drop safes, time release safes, remotely controlled door locks, panic buttons or microphones both in and outside the facility for emergency calls** — Additional security devices are becoming commonplace in many companies. More and more drive-through windows in fast food restaurants contain bullet proof glass and cash exchange boxes. Restaurants and convenience stores are installing drop safes that cannot be opened by employees, and which allow only a minimum of cash to be accessed at any one time. Security hardware makes employees feel more secure and helps to support management in their contention that they are attempting to provide a "safe" workplace and may be a necessary piece of evidence in any lawsuits that arise from a criminal act committed on the premises. Security hardware alone, however, will do little to stop those perpetrators who are completely irrational and do not care if others see and/or record the crime. Illustration 8b is a proposed Security Inspection Checklist which might be adapted to most business concerns, and 8c outlines Telephone Procedures in case of a phoned-in bomb threat.

In a nutshell, preventative strategies should:

1) <u>Increase the effort</u> required by a criminal to commit his intended crime by physical barriers, security hardware and properly trained personnel;

2) <u>Increase the risks</u> of detection, identification, capture and even injury to the criminal; and

3) <u>Reduce the rewards</u>. If robbery is the motive and very little cash or valuable property is readily available, it probably won't be worth the effort or the risk involved. If personal injury is the intent, well protected and trained employees are less likely to be harmed.

The conclusion that can be drawn from all of the above is that company policies and procedures, employee training, and security personnel and hardware must all be closely linked together to form a chain of defense measures designed to reduce and control violent acts in the workplace. Besides protecting employees and customers alike, these suggestions, when implemented, provide a positive response to "premises' liability" lawsuits brought by injured or traumatized employees, customers, or family members of victims. While it is not possible to totally prevent all violent acts at work, employees can be trained to respond in a manner that will increase their odds of survival. To ignore the rising numbers of violent incidents in the workplace today could be viewed as a callus lack of concern for the safety and well being of employees and customers. This is a posture no business can afford to take.

PERSONALITY TRAITS OF "LOW SELF-CONTROL" INDIVIDUALS

* Tendency to respond to tangible stimuli in the immediate environment . . . "here and now" gratification orientation.

* Tendency to lack diligence, tenacity or persistence in executing a plan . . . orientation to simple tasks that do not require premeditation.

* Tendency to be "adventuresome" rather than calculating . . . criminal acts are risky, thrilling or exciting.

* Tendency to prefer physical activity/contact rather than cognitive or mental activity . . . violence satisfies emotional needs that cannot be satisfied by normal behavior."

* Tendency to be very self-centered, indifferent/insensitive to others . . . little or no awareness of rights of others, violence does not have emotional consequences.

* Tendency to become frustrated, minimal tolerance for delayed gratification or confusion . . . very violent temper that is not controllable and may erupt with little or no provocation.

* Tendency to respond to conflict/confrontation through physical acts rather than verbal . . . action oriented and very difficult to negotiate within crisis situation.

Illustration 8a
Sources: Gottfredson and Hirsch, 1990 and Grasmick, Tittle, Bursik and Arneklev, 1993.

ULTIMATE SURVIVORS
SECURITY INSPECTION CHECKLIST

Facility/Location_____

Present Security Staff ____Yes ____No _____ Armed ____Unarmed
 ____Uniformed ____#/shift _____

 _____Comments

Designated Responsibilities: _____

Security Reports to: _____ Daily Security Checklist?_____

Weapons Policy ____Yes ____No   Parcels in & out ____Yes ____No

Parking Lot checks ____Yes ___No #/shift ____ Est. time for ck?_____

Responsible for change of locks or codes or notification upon terminations?

_____

How security risks observed are reported & to whom _____

_____

Procedure for securing facilities _____

Outside Lighting

Area A _____ Type_____ Adquate?_____

Area B _____ Type_____ Adequate?_____

Area C _____ Type_____ Adequate?_____

Outside Panic Alarm, Callbox or Surveillance Camera –
Constant Monitor?_____

Area A_____ Type_____ Adequate?_____

Area B_____ Type_____ Adequate?_____

Area C_____ Type_____ Adequate?_____

Locked or Restricted Access to Parking Lots

Area A_____ Comments_____

Area B_____ Comments_____

Area C_____ Comments_____

 # Of Outside Entrances to Building

Bldg. A_____ #_____ # Always Locked from Outside____

# of People w/keys, cards or codes ___ # of People exiting locked doors___

Reasons why _____ Comments_____

Bldg. B_____ #_____ # Always Locked from Outside____

# of People w/keys, cards or codes ___ # of People exiting locked doors ___

Reasons why _____ Comments_____

Bldg. C_____ #_____ # Always Locked from Outside ____

Illustration 8b
(1of 2)

# of People w/keys, cards or codes ___ # of People exiting locked doors ___
Reasons why_____ Comments_____
Designated Employee entrance & exit? __Yes __No Timeclock?__ All?__
Policy regarding off-duty employees on premises _____Yes _____No
Policy regarding inside access by visitors _____Yes _____No
Comments_____
Locked restrooms - Bldg. A_____ Bldg. B_____ Bldg. C_____
Restroom checks at end of each shift: Bldg. A_____ Bldg. B_____ Bldg. C___
Front Desk Area
Auto. door locks___Yes ___No. Remote Speaker/Bell_____Yes _____No
Buzzer/gated access to offices from reception area _____Yes _____No.
Window/camera for visibility - looking out ___Good ___Poor ____None
                        looking in ___Good ___Poor ____None
Emergency alarm ___Yes ___No Silent?____ Notifies?_____
Front desk area on constantly monitored surveillance camera ___Yes ___No
Other protection (i.e. bullet proof glass, etc.) _____
Bomb Threat Policy _____Yes _____No Form presented_____
Reception personnel notified of terminations and security risk __Yes __No
General Office Area
Visibility ref. shelving, displays or partitions _____Good _____Poor
Comments_____
Surveillance Cameras _____Yes _____No
Critical Records Security _____Yes _____No
Factory/shop/production work area
Visibility ref. shelving, displays, equip. or partitions _____Good _____Poor
Surveillance Cameras _____Yes _____No
Critical Equipment Security _____Yes _____No
Currency or Securities policies
Drop safe or other on premises ___Yes ___No Limited Access?_____
Bank runs procedure - Irregular schedule ___ # of Different Persons____
Emergency procedure and policies training for all employees
Written policies distributed _____Yes _____No
Oral lectures and training _____Yes _____No
Mandated for all employees _____Yes _____No
Offered, but not mandated _____Yes _____No
Hands-On Self-defense training offered ____Yes _____No
                        Mandated?_____
Current procedure for employees to notify management of workplace violence risk or incident:_____
Form_____ E-mail_____ Phone_____

Illustration 8b
Prepared by Ultimate Survivors, Inc.

BOMB THREAT CHECK LIST
Telephone Procedures

INSTRUCTIONS: Be calm. Be courteous. *Listen*, do not interrupt the caller. Notify supervisor by prearranged signal while caller is on the line.

Name of Operator_____ Time_____ Date_____

Caller's Identity: Name if known, or given _____

Sex: __Male __Female __Adult __Juvenile Approx. Age ___Years

ORIGIN OF CALL:

_____Local _____Long Distance _____Booth _____Internal

(From within bldg.?) If internal note where call is coming from, if known

_____

VOICE CHARACTERISTICS		SPEECH	
___Loud	___Soft	___Fast	___Slow
___High Pitch	___Deep	___Distinct	___Distorted
___Raspy	___Pleasant	___Stutter	___Nasal
___Intoxicated	___Disguised	___Slurred	___Lisp
	_____Other		_____Other

LANGUAGE SKILLS		ACCENT
_____Excellent	_____Good	_____Local
_____Fair	_____Poor	_____Not Local
_____Technical		_____Region
	_____Other	_____Foreign
		_____Race

MANNER		BACKGROUND NOISES	
___Calm	___Angry	___Factory Machines	___Trains
___Rational	___Irrational	___Bedlam	___Animals
___Coherent	___Incoherent	___Music	___Quiet
___Deliberate	___Emotional	___Office Machines	___Voices
___Righteous	___Laughing	___Street/Traffic	___Party
	_____Other	___Mixed	_____Other

Illustration 8c
(1 of 2)

BOMB THREAT CHECKLIST (continued)

<u>Procedure</u>: Pretend difficulty with hearing. *Keep caller talking.* Attempt to question caller as follows:

"When will it go off?" Certain Hour _____ Time Remaining _____

"Where is it located?" Building _____ Area _____

"What kind of bomb?" _____

"Where are you (bomber) now?"_____

"How do you know so much about the bomb?" _____

"Who are you and where are you now?" _____

<u>If the building is occupied, inform caller that detonation could cause injury or death.</u> Note whether the caller appeared familiar with the plant or building by his description of the bomb location. Write out the message in its entirety and any other comments on a separate sheet of paper and attach to this check list. Notify your supervisor as instructed. Talk to no one other than instructed by your supervisor and police.

Illustration 8c
Prepared by Ultimate Survivors, Inc.

Robbery Prevention and Victim Survival

*T*he objectives here are two-fold: First, we hope that by providing suggestions and information we may help citizens avoid becoming robbery victims; and secondly, if in spite of all their precautions they are still accosted, to improve their chances of survival. This is best facilitated with a thorough understanding of the prevalence and nature of the crime. A "robbery" is defined as:

> "The felonious and forcible taking of property from the care, custody or control of a person or persons, against his/their will, by violence, or by putting the person(s) in fear (whether armed or "strong-arm")."

In order for the crime of robbery to take place, the victim *must be present* — unlike many burglaries, for instance, where the victim may *not* be present.

The crime of robbery has probably "evolved" and changed more in character during the past ten years than any other violent offense. Ten years ago only about 1 in 10 robbery offenders was a juvenile. Now, more than 6 in 10 are committed by juveniles. We now find more robberies committed by multiple assailants, as youthful gang members find their "bravery" bolstered by forming a "pack". The *reasons* for robberies have changed also. Real economic need or desire are more and more often not the motivation, but instead ego gratification, power trips, gang initiation, revenge or support of a drug habit may be the underlying reason for the robbery.

August, October and December are often the worst months for robberies, but certainly they can take place anywhere, anytime. Most robberies and assaults with an armed offender take place at night, between 6:00 P.M. and midnight, according to the Bureau of Justice Statistics. As we stated in Chapter Six, carjackings are more likely to occur during this same time period.

Let's talk about the risk to you. The National Crime Victimization Survey published in May, 1995 by the Bureau of Justice Statistics stated that more than 6 out of every 1,000 Americans will be victims of a completed or attempted robbery. In addition, two-thirds of the robberies will be completed with property taken, and nearly one-third of all robbery victims will be injured in the process. There were more than *1.3 million* robberies reported in 1993.

While approximately 82% of all robberies are committed by strangers, you are more likely to be injured by an assailant who is an acquaintance, if he believes you can identify him to police.

Should you take some self-protective actions such as fighting, running or resisting in some way? Only you can assess the risk of a violent confrontation if/when it occurs, but the general rule of thumb for a robbery victim is as follows: If the perpetrator wants your *property,* i.e. a car, money, jewelry, purse, etc., — *give it to him.* Your property can be replaced, don't risk your life for it! If, however, it is *you* he wants, you may very well have to resist.

Suggested actions to prevent or survive a robbery are as follows:

Preventative Measures:

1. At night, stay in well-lighted areas.

2. Avoid solo travel as much as possible, especially at night.

3. Have a plan in case of emergency. Know what you can *and will* do.

4. Travel light and avoid carrying purses, briefcases or parcels which tie up your hands and your attention, and which indicate you have something of value. Don't carry anything you can't bear to lose. Avoid flashy jewelry.

5. Don't dress like a victim — avoid restrictive or bulky clothing and fragile footwear. Be sure you *look* like you could run and/or fight effectively.

6. Stay alert —be aware of your surroundings. Avoid possible problem areas (notice suspicious cars or vans, people sitting in cars or outside the business you want to go into, groups of unruly individuals, etc.)

7. A commercial business should avoid posters or displays that block windows or that restrict the ability of employees, law enforcement officers, or potential customers to see clearly from the inside looking out or the outside looking in the building.

8. Pay attention to activities in the parking lot if possible. Call the police if suspicious persons or vehicles are present.

9. Be unpredictable or use an *irregular* schedule for taking out trash, leaving the premises with cash or receipts, or making deposits. These activities are best done in pairs or with a security guard present. (Trash is, unfortunately, usually dumped out of a back entrance at the end of the day when the receipts are predictably being counted, and is a "weak spot" favored by robbers.)

10. Keep restrooms locked, if possible, and make certain that people who go in *come out!* Removable ceiling tiles in restrooms are often repositories for weapons and drugs, and should be checked regularly.

11. Pay particular attention to "customers" that come in at or near closing time and seem disinclined to leave.

12. Don't be afraid to call police if you are concerned or suspicious. Better to call them and not need them, than to need them and not have called them.

If A Robbery Occurs:

1. Compliance with dignity is the key. Try to stay calm and maintain your dignity and self control. The more agitated *you* are, the more excited, agitated and aggressive your assailant may become.

2. If you are working in a commercial business, activate silent alarm and cameras, *if you can do so unobserved.*

3. Be observant. (This will help you to stay calm.) Note specific details concerning assailant(s) such as scars, jewelry, tattoos, bad teeth, clothing, manner of speaking

(accent, tone, gruff, husky, slurred, etc.), approximate size, weight, and age, hair (including facial hair, length, style and color), etc.

4. Go "Hollywood". Raise your arms — This attracts attention and yet indicates to the perpetrator that you are "cooperating" with the "universally recognized response" of a robbery victim. This will also begin a dialogue between you and the attacker who will probably ask you to put your hands down. This has a dual benefit: First, it is hard to shoot or strike while carrying on a conversation (you can calmly explain that you are attempting to cooperate with him and ask him what he wants you to do — keep him talking.) Secondly, it places you in the proper position for a disarming technique, if necessary at that time, as described and illustrated in Chapter Seven.

5. Stay near windows and/or video camera, if possible, if you are inside a commercial establishment.

6. Move away from other victims, if present, slowly and unobtrusively. Don't cluster or make it easy for the perpetrator to herd you into a controllable and/or easily extinguished group.

7. If it is money or personal property (such as jewelry, wallets or purses) that the robber wants — give it to him slowly. Do not rush — no fast movements. If you have bait money (specially marked bills), give it to him, even if he says not to. (He can't tell).

8. Try to keep any prepared note by the robber (accidentally drop it on the floor, or slip it in your pocket when he isn't looking).

9. If he seems satisfied, takes what he wants and leaves swiftly, watch his retreat and see what he does, i.e., did he get into a vehicle, leave on foot, what was his direction of travel, were there any accomplices?

A decision to resist, run or fight may be influenced by the following "red flag situations":

a) A weapon is present and has already been used. (Willingness to use violence has already been demonstrated.)

b) Robber or assailant is known to one or more of the victims.

c) Robber or assailant makes no effort to hide his identity.

d) Robber or assailant is in no hurry to leave; stays to taunt or abuse victims.

e) Apparent mental instability, confusion, disorientation or apparent lack of planning of perpetrator or the obvious use of drugs or alcohol by the perpetrator.

f) Anger or hostility appears to escalate and/or any victim is attacked.

g) Robber instructs victim(s) to go to back room, freezer, vault, etc., or to kneel down, be tied up, blindfolded or leave with perpetrator as a kidnap victim or hostage. Your odds of survival go down dramatically as the area and your physical freedom of movement are reduced.

Suggested actions after a robbery:

1. Activate alarm if it has not already been done. Be sure everyone on the premises knows there has been a robbery.

2. Lock all doors until police arrive.

3. Notify all of the following by telephone and tell them the robber has left, giving descriptions and direction of travel:

    a. Police Department (if inside city limits)

    b. Sheriff's Office

    c. FBI — if appropriate (for a bank robbery, kidnapping, etc.)

    d. Corporate Headquarters or other appropriate emergency number (if a commercial entity is involved).

4. Keep people out of the crime scene area and preserve any possible evidence such as fingerprints, items dropped or discarded by the robber, etc.

5. Identify all witnesses, including customers, and ask them to remain until law enforcement authorities arrive.

6. Immediately write down what <u>you</u> observed and heard. Put the date, time and your name on it. <u>Do not</u> compare notes with any other victims, who should be asked to do the same. This will save time when the police arrive and is more likely to be recounted properly immediately after the incident rather than at a later time.

7. Remain calm! It's over and *you survived it!* It is normal to be very emotional and shaken after such an ordeal, even if you managed to be a "rock" during it.

CHAPTER NINE

CRIMES AGAINST
SENIOR CITIZENS

Likelihood of Victimization

The elderly comprise the fastest growing segment of the U.S. population, and as the "baby boomers" rapidly add to this group, more attention is being focused on their protection and well being. As Americans live longer and are more active than their predecessors, they are naturally more likely to be exposed to the criminal elements in our society. While it is true that older persons are generally less likely to be violent crime victims than younger people, they are much more likely to sustain serious injuries when a victimization *does* occur.

It is, therefore, important to identify when, where and how these older citizens are being victimized, and recognize factors that tend to increase their vulnerability. According to the Bureau of Justice Statistics 1993 National Crime Victimization Survey, the violent crime victimization rate is 1 in 179 persons for those 65 and older. This includes rapes and/or sexual assaults, robberies and assaults. An October, 1992 B.J.S. Special Report entitled "Elderly Victims" stated that while the overall victimization rate for crimes of *violence* for persons under age 25 was nearly 16 times higher than for persons over age 65, *personal larcenies* (such as purse snatching and pocket picking) did not reflect this pattern. Those who were 65 or older were about as likely as those under age 65 to be victims of personal larceny which involved contact. Household crimes such as burglary, household larceny and motor vehicle theft were less likely to be committed against the elderly, however the victimization rate was still nearly 80 per 1000 persons over age 65.

The elderly appear to be particularly susceptible to crimes motivated by economic gain such as fraud or "con" games, robbery, personal and household larceny, and burglary. For younger age groups, we find that assault rates are nearly four times higher than robbery rates, but among the elderly the likelihood of robbery is about the same as that of an assault, with *38% of violent crime victimizations against the elderly being robberies.* Most *homicide* victims 65 years of age or older were killed during the commission of another felony, such as a robbery. Recent studies indicate that elderly victims are more likely than younger victims to face offenders armed with guns, and are more likely than other victims to have been robbed by a stranger or multiple offenders. The percentage of *assaults* committed by strangers was not significantly different between elderly victims and their younger counterparts.

The elderly are almost twice as likely as younger victims to be victimized at or near their homes. This undoubtedly reflects their lifestyle, which in turn affects their vulnerability to certain crimes. They are more likely to live alone and stay at their residence more often because they are retired or not working at a full time job, and they are less likely to participate regularly in activities after dark. Victimizations "on the street" are the next most likely place of occurrence for elderly victims. For the overall category of violent crimes and for the specific crimes of robbery and assault, victims age 75 or older were more likely to be victimized at home than elsewhere, while those between the ages of 65 and 74 were more likely to be victimized on the street. A higher percentage of those age 75 or older were victims of violent crime in commercial or public establishments, compared to those age 65 to 74.

For crimes of violence and household crimes, elderly males are generally more likely to have higher victimization rates than elderly females, however the women are more likely to be victims of personal larceny with contact, such as purse snatching. In addition, the 1994 Mother's Day Report released by the Older Women's League stated that one million older women each year suffer violence in or outside their homes. Their report further stated that every year approximately one in 100 women aged 50 - 64 becomes a victim of violent crime, with 40% of these acts being committed by family or people they know. Twice as many over-65 women are mugged at or near their homes as younger women, with three-fourths of these victimizations happening during the daytime. The murder rate for women 65 and older increased 30% in the period

1974–1990, according to this report, with the rate for men the same age dropping 6%.

Elderly persons who are either separated or divorced have the highest rates of victimization for all types of crime compared to any other marital status. Those residing in cities compared to either suburban or rural elderly also showed higher violent crime rates, however *rural* elderly were more likely to experience *household* crimes in general and burglary in particular, compared to those elderly residing in suburban areas. Elderly *renters* are significantly more likely to experience all forms of *personal crime* including robbery, simple assault, and personal theft, however elderly homeowners are more likely than renters to become victims of *household crimes* such as burglary and motor vehicle theft.

Income appears to be a factor with the elderly, as it is with younger members of society. Those with annual incomes under $7,500 were more likely to experience *violent* crimes such as aggravated assaults and robberies than those elderly with higher family incomes. Those with the highest incomes ($25,000 or more), however, were more likely to experience a *personal* crime of theft such as purse snatching, or a *household* crime such as burglary. Education level is usually interconnected with an individual's income, which may in turn be related to marital status and to place of residence, all of which affects vulnerability to certain types of crime.

Perhaps not surprisingly, elderly victims of violent crime are less likely to take self-protective action than were younger victims, which undoubtedly contributes to their vulnerability in the eyes of criminal predators. While violent crime victims under the age of 65 took self-protective actions 73% of the time, those over 65 initiated these actions in only 58% of the cases. Of those elderly who took self-protective measures, they were less likely than their younger counterparts to use *physical* action such as attacking, chasing the offender, or physically resisting in some other way. Additionally, it would be generally expected that many of their efforts might have been less effective than those enacted by younger, stronger, more agile victims. That is precisely why the suggestions and techniques which are presented later in this chapter were developed, with the specific abilities and limitations of the older population in mind.

In addition to the crime prevention measures listed in Chapter One, the following suggestions are made with the elderly in mind.

* If you use public transportation, use only busy, well-lighted stops.

* Don't fall asleep or day dream during a ride on public transportation or in a public place. Stay alert!

* Pay close attention to who else gets on or off the bus, cab or subway with you. If you feel uneasy, walk directly to a place where there are other people, or get back on the public transportation and ask for help.

* Don't keep large amounts of cash at home.

* Use Direct Deposit for Social Security or pension checks.

* Avoid displaying large amounts of cash or other tempting targets such as expensive jewelry.

* Work out a buddy system with a nearby friend or trusted neighbor and check on each other frequently.

* Be alert to news reports about crimes committed in your area.

* Join a Neighborhood Watch group.

Con Games and Swindles

W hile frauds of all types are perpetrated on virtually every segment of the population, many schemes are directed specifically at older citizens in an effort to bilk them out of as much of their money as possible. The elderly and retired are frequently easy to reach in person or by phone at their residence, and are often lonely enough to strike up a conversation with a friendly stranger, particularly one who seems eager to "help" them or "give" them something. Once the unscrupulous pitchman gets a foot in the door, so to speak, they normally will continue the "relationship" with one scheme after another until the unwitting victim runs out of money or finally refuses to give them any more. In spite of the fact that these deceptive practices are extremely prevalent, they are so diverse and sporadically reported, (the victim often doesn't know for some time, if ever, that he or she has been defrauded) that they are difficult to prosecute, even if a victim complains.

Sadly, there appears to be no uniform, standard definition for these categories of crimes. This legislative deficiency impedes investigative and prosecutorial efforts by local, state or federal authorities, and fails to provide firm penalties for those who commit them. Not only do these loopholes in the existing laws allow for these frauds to continue, but no solid numbers exist for how many individuals are actually victimized each year because, unlike other major crime categories such as burglaries, robberies, assaults and thefts, frauds are not a category of crime that is reported on annual, standardized law enforcement reporting forms.

Crime prevention experts agree that, although no one can accurately say exactly how many of these swindles and frauds are perpetrated each year, con games are by far a greater danger to the financial security of the elderly than any other category of crime. Presently, the only defense against these crimes is to recognize them and refuse to be suckered or sweet-talked by a fast-talking, hard-pressure sales person, even one who seems nice and polite.

Telemarketing is a huge industry, and is used to promote nearly everything these days. Con artists have, of course, jumped on the bandwagon and "poisoned the pot". An estimated 14,000 fraudulent telemarketing businesses are operating nationwide and are now a $40 billion drain on the pocketbooks of Americans, many of them older citizens. A recent survey indicated that *at least* 10% of all telemarketing calls are scams, and since most are made from out of state or even out of the country, prosecution is difficult if not impossible, even if the perpetrator can be identified (which is often no small chore). When you are thinking how "sincere" someone sounds promoting some cause or "deal", just remember that they are getting a percentage of whatever you spend, so their "sincerity" is financially motivated. Don't be pressured into buying something as a result of a random telemarketing call, and don't be afraid to be rude or hang up on the caller. _They_ are the ones intruding upon _your_ privacy, and using _your_ phone line to promote _their_ business!

Some of these telemarketing schemes involve offering a "free" gift or trip, but require a "handling fee" and ask you to verify a credit card number and expiration date. Do not give your credit card numbers out to unknown individuals over the phone. No *legitimate* company asks you to *pay* anything for a prize you have won. You should not have to pay up front for taxes, handling, or accounting fees. Nor should you have to pay anything to "increase your chances" of winning. The old saw "You don't get something for nothing" is still true.

Beware of requests to send money or use a credit card to buy something sight unseen, unless you initiated the call. Be especially cautious if a caller offers to send someone to your home to pick up a payment, or rushes you for a decision on a purchase. Legitimate businesses are unlikely to pressure you or insist you act immediately.

Offers to enter out of state lotteries with the use of your credit card are another ploy. If you want to participate in an out of state lottery, get someone you know and trust to buy the tickets for you and mail them to you — or better yet, don't spend any limited resources on gambling enterprises. You should be extremely cautious of anything that sounds too good to be true.

Senior citizens are often targeted by salesmen offering extra health insurance, claiming that the existing policy and Medicare won't cover nursing home care. Funeral and burial policies are another way some calculating individuals wring unnecessary dollars from the elderly, preying on their concern for the loved ones they leave behind who will be "too bereaved" to make sensible choices after their death. Having these details prepared in advance is a valid idea, but have your family present and let them participate in these decisions and know your wishes. With the family present there is less likelihood of pressure sales and unnecessary "add-ons".

The **Charity Racket** is another common telemarketing scheme. The cause often sounds very worthy and the solicitor seems sincere, but what do you know about the distribution of funds donated to this charity? Recent investigations into even some of the most "reputable" and well-known charities revealed "administrative costs" of *more than 90%*, which, of course, were paid first, before the balance, if any, was applied to the cause of the needy recipients. In addition, shady solicitors often deliberately choose names for their organizations that are intended to *sound like* legitimate charities.

Before you give, ask for identification of the caller, get the exact name of the charity, and ask for written information about the charity's purpose, how funds are used, what percent goes to administrative costs, and if contributions are tax deductible. Check with the Better Business Bureau in your area to determine if this charity is authorized to solicit in your state. If you are not satisfied with the answers and feel something isn't quite right, don't give.

In general, do not allow any phone solicitor to pressure you into making an immediate financial decision of any kind, even for a small amount of money. If you are not willing or able to just tell them "No thanks!", then tell them that you (a) want to think it over for a few days; (b) need to talk to your children and lawyer before you decide; or (c) want to check first with the Police Department or Better Business Bureau, or both. If they are legitimate, they will respect your wishes and welcome your investigation of their business practices. If not, you probably won't hear from them again, although some obnoxious telephone solicitors will bother you again and again until you threaten to sue them.

Other common con games frequently employed are numerous variations of the following:

The Pigeon Drop. This often takes place in a parking lot or shopping mall. Two strangers who claim not to know each other tell you they've found a large sum of money or other valuables. They offer to split the loot with you if everyone involved puts up "good faith" money. They may offer to go with you to your bank so that you can withdraw the cash. After you turn over your cash, you will never see it or the strangers again.

A recent variation of this theme involves a "very professional" looking woman (she may even have business cards) who stops you to ask where a certain church or bank is. She will tell you she is new in town and came to donate a large sum of money (she may show it to you) but needs help finding the object of her generosity. She will ask you to accompany her since she is afraid to be alone with all that money. Once you leave with her, the scenario can take any number of turns, including a robbery situation. She always works with at least one or two partners, often drives a vehicle with out of state tags (usually rented), and has a variety of identities.

Bottom line: *never leave with a stranger.* If you feel you must be helpful, offer to call the police for her. The odds are that suggestion will send her packing fast.

The Bank Examiner Scam. In this racket a so-called bank official asks for your help to catch a dishonest teller. He asks you to withdraw money from your account and turn it over to him so he can check the serial numbers. You do this and you get a receipt, but your cash is gone. Remember that no legitimate bank official would ever ask you to withdraw your own money for such a project.

The Pyramid Scheme. Here someone offers you an effortless, "sure-fire" way to make money. The way it works is you are asked to invest a certain amount and solicit others to do the same. They in turn solicit additional people, and so on like a chain letter. Sometimes the initial investors are paid a small dividend, but when the pyramid crashes, *and it always does*, everyone loses *except* the person at the top of the pyramid who has taken everyone's money. These schemes are illegal in almost every state, but due to greed and ignorance about them, people involved usually lose a lot of money before they fold or are reported to the police and investigated.

The Funeral Chaser. The human parasites that use this ploy function in the following manner. Shortly after the death of a relative, an expensive leather-bound Bible is delivered which allegedly was ordered by your dearly departed. Or perhaps you will receive a statement in the mail for an expensive item on which you are now asked to make payments. The Funeral Chaser uses obituary notices to target and prey on bereaved families. Don't be fooled. *You are not responsible for someone else's purchases,* and all legitimate claims will be settled by the estate.

Bait and Switch. This scheme is used frequently by many unscrupulous retailers who target gullible customers of all ages. Basically, the plan is to offer some item free or at a ridiculously low price as a "come on" to get people to come into their businesses. Once there, the unwitting customers will be told that they are "out" of the original item, and they will be offered another, "better", more expensive replacement which will cost the customer additional money, and which is usually grossly overpriced. Be prepared to walk out swiftly anytime you are faced with this type of false advertising, or insist that they give you a written "rain check" for the item that was advertised at the low price.

The top five **postal scams** according to the U.S. Postal Inspection Service, were compiled after 416,216 complaints in one year. They state that the five biggest lies told to consumers by mail are:

1) "You are a guaranteed winner of a valuable prize." This ploy asks the so-called winner to pay for chemically inert "vitamins", cheap home security systems and water purifiers, or contribute to a fake charity, before getting what turns out to be a booby prize.

2) "This chain letter is legal." The inspectors say that sooner or later everyone gets one of these, but after you pay for copying and mailing out letters, it's one of life's biggest losers. Also, *any* chain letter that asks for money is *illegal* when sent through the mail.

3) "Stuff envelopes at home and earn big money." These scams ask victims to send money for a "plan". This is the plan: Send out letters asking people to send money for a plan!

4) "Your humble assistance is highly solicited in transferring millions of dollars, available from the Nigerian National Petroleum
Company, to share with your good self. All we need is your
bank account number." The scam is to get some advance
money from the victim, sort of a pigeon-drop via the mail. The
good faith money quickly disappears, of course. Formerly targeted at businesses, this scam is now being used on individuals
at home.

5) "You've been selected to receive a fabulous vacation." You pay
a one-time membership fee or handling charge, the offer claims.
Inspectors say, however, that the vacation can turn into a nightmare of scheduling problems, shabby hotels and nonexistent
cruises that leave vacationers standing on the dock.

If you should receive actual, cashable **unsolicited checks** in the
mail, usually for about $5.00, before you endorse and cash them,
read the small print. It will normally say something like "must be
endorsed with recipient's name and checking account number. The
checking account number is requested so that the firm can debit the
consumer's bank account automatically for annual or semi-annual
fees that may amount to several hundreds of dollars. This is an
alarming new scheme called the "automatic debit scam", involving
the illegal use of bank checking account numbers to drain the
accounts. It is perpetrated by Canadian con artists using long distance telephone lines to reach across an international border and
above the heads of American law enforcement agents.

Because many older citizens cannot read extremely fine, small
print, they do not realize that they are providing information for a
"demand draft" which is processed much like a check, with one
important exception - it does not require your signature and is
automatically processed by the bank with no questions asked. The
bank assumes the drafter would not have your checking account
number unless you intended him to use it for payment by demand
draft from your account. Guard your checking account number.

Beware of **free inspections** that uncover "needed" repairs that
will cost thousands of dollars, or **half-price deals** offered by con-
tractors who come to your home and tell you they have materials

"left over" from a nearby job. These are common tricks used by dishonest firms or individuals who try to talk vulnerable home-owners into getting work done that they don't need. Always get several estimates for any major work, and don't be pressured into accepting a one-day-only offer. Ask for references and check them out. If you do decide to have the work done, get a written contract and make sure you understand all its provisions. *Never* pay in advance of the work being done. Withhold payment until the job is completed. Pay by check, not with cash, and ask for a receipt of payment.

In summary, be suspicious of anyone who offers you a chance for a "get rich quick" opportunity which requires an investment or good faith money; investments that promise unusually high returns; bargains on home repairs or supplemental health insurance. In addition, never make cash transactions in secret. Discuss any large transaction with your banker, accountant or financial adviser.

Be wary of exaggerated claims for health and medical products, such as "miracle cures" for cancer or arthritis, hair restorers, quick weight loss, or glasses and hearing aids at bargain prices from unknown sources. Before buying anything of this nature, check with your doctor, pharmacist or clinic.

Never give details about your credit cards to phone solicitors, even if they offer you gifts, a free vacation, or a sweepstakes prize. Be suspicious of high pressure sales tactics. If you shop by mail, use only companies that you know are reputable. Never buy real estate sight unseen. Ask for the HUD report if the property is being advertised interstate.

Keep a tight rein on your finances and don't give credit cards, checkbooks, savings account passbooks or negotiable documents to your housekeeper or caretaker. Don't make an employee a joint owner of your bank account or your property. Be wary of someone claiming you owe money for an item ordered by a deceased rela-tive, or trying to convince you that you have *forgotten* ordering something yourself. Door-to-door sales, telephone sales and work-at-home schemes should all be checked out by your local or state consumer protection agency.

If you believe you have been scammed or swindled, don't be hesitant to call the police and the National Fraud Information Center at (800) 876-7060. At the very least, they can make the public aware of what is going on and try to prevent more victimizations. They might even be able to actually prosecute the individuals in some cases. An attorney can advise you if a civil suit would be likely to recover any of your losses.

Physical Defenses for Seniors

*I*t has been our experience that most individuals are capable of performing the majority of the techniques previously described well into their eighties or beyond, and we have had many self-defense students that were "awesome" at that age. It is also true, however, that as we age we may lose some bone density, some muscle strength, some quickness of response, and our coordination may not be what it once was. Our hearing and eyesight may also be slightly diminished. All this certainly *does not* mean that as we get older we become helpless, nor are we unable to function efficiently to protect ourselves, if necessary. It *does* mean that as we age we need to be *more prepared* and *more aware of our surroundings*, perhaps, than our younger counterparts.

Since everyone has different capabilities and personal strengths and weaknesses, it is recommended that seniors review the chapters on Prevention and Preparation and Self Defense Theory to select those suggestions and techniques that are most useful to them, personally. Particular attention should be paid to the suggestions regarding avoidance of purses and flashy jewelry, solo travel, and "fat" wallets in an obvious pocket. In addition, if traveling with one or more friends, take care not to get so involved in a conversation that you lose track of what is going on around you. Being aware of a possible or potential threat is paramount to avoiding and/or surviving it. Become a "people watcher", if you are not already one, both in and out of your home.

No one should ever have to endure being manhandled or physically abused, regardless of their age or situation, and appropriate defensive maneuvers should be taken if this should ever occur. Finger jabs to the eyes take no special strength and can easily be administered by young and old alike. Elbow and knee strikes, foot stomps and head butts are also previously mentioned techniques which are easily employed and require very little strength or skill.

Some simple grappling techniques are demonstrated in the illustration photos at the end of this section. There are two good defense choices for a "two handed grab". The first is called a "push/pull" exercise. The "victim" simultaneously draws in one hand (usually the "strong" hand), and forcefully extends the other in a palm strike directed at the jaw or nose of the assailant, as shown in illustration 9a and 9b. The second alternative for the "victim" is to raise the elbow of their "strong" arm and cross over both assailant's arms, drawing their face into "target" range for an elbow strike. (See Illustration 9c and 9d).

A forward (face to face) choke hold can be defeated as follows. Bring your arms up over your assailants, cross them, and bring them down hard to your chest, trapping your assailant's arms and causing him to drop, bringing his eyes into striking range of your fingers. (Illustrations 9e-g).

A rear choke is normally a much more serious threat than one that is face to face. The first thing you must do is be able to breathe. Dig your fingers into the assailant's arm (use arm hair if necessary) to peel their arm away from your windpipe. Immediately duck your chin to prevent them from again placing their arm against your windpipe. (They can't choke a chin! They can, however, apply some uncomfortable pressure.) Next, use your elbow for a hard rear strike to their stomach, ribs or groin. Now you can stomp a foot, kick a shin, go for the eyes, etc. (See Illustrations 9h - 9k).

One of the possible "advantages" of age is that we may be carrying a cane or using a crutch or walker. These items, along with something we all carry from time to time, an umbrella, can become very useful unconventional "weapons" in an emergency. As shown in Illustration 9l -9n, a cane, crutch, club, or baton can be used in an effective "two strike" succession across the collarbone and the kneecaps to incapacitate the attackers arm and leg, followed by a forceful thrust to the abdomen or midsection with the end of the weapon.

These items can also be used is as a "trip" mechanism when placed firmly behind an assailant's knees. As shown in Illustrations 9o - 9p, a slight upward tug as you lean into your assailant will cause him to fall hard to the ground. Additionally, from a clothes grab or choke hold, one can bring the cane or umbrella down hard across the radial nerves on the wrists and arms of the assailant, and in a continuous sweeping motion as he is forced downward, directly up into their throat, as shown in Illustrations 9q - 9s.

A crutch, because of its length and strength, is also effective as a "stomping", "striking", "poking" and "tripping" tool. Any of the items mentioned can also be used to block punches or kicks, and can, with a little creativity, be used on most of the vital targets mentioned in Chapter Three.

Once again, we would like to point out that these suggested defense techniques are only proposed for "worst case scenario" situations. Property such as purses and wallets are not worth being injured or killed to protect their contents. If your *life* is at risk, however, you must take self protective actions. While the prospect of a physical confrontation is unpleasant, it is somewhat comforting to know *how* to defend yourself if such an event occurs. Since every individual and every situation is different, it behooves us to consider as many defense options as possible. Being well prepared is the best possible defense.

ILLUS. 9A

1 of 2

Demonstration of "Push/pull" grappling defense

ILLUS. 9B

2 of 2

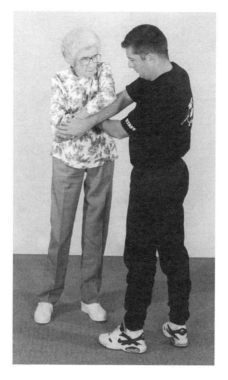

*Demonstration
of "cross-over
with elbow
strike" grappling
defense*

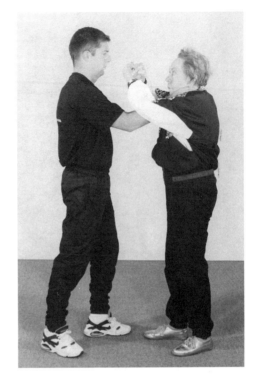

ILLUS. 9E

1 of 3

Bring arms up over assailant"s arms

"Choke hold" defense

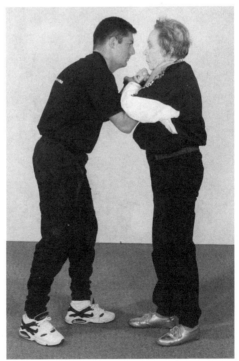

ILLUS. 9F

2 of 3

Cross arms and bring down hard to your chest

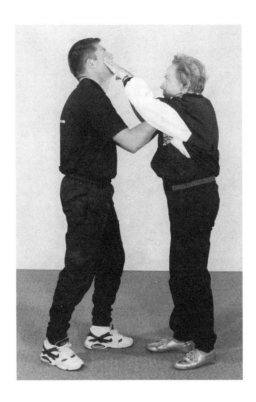

3 of 3

Finish with eye strike

ILLUS. 9H

1 of 4

Pry arm away from throat

rear choke defense

ILLUS. 9I

2 of 4

Tuck chin into chest

ILLUS. 9J

3 of 4

Execute rear elbow strike

ILLUS. 9K

4 of 4

Follow up with foot stomp, eye jab, etc.

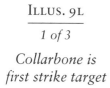

ILLUS. 9L

1 of 3

Collarbone is first strike target

Demonstration of strike zones for cane, crutch, baton or club

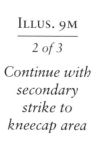

ILLUS. 9M

2 of 3

Continue with secondary strike to kneecap area

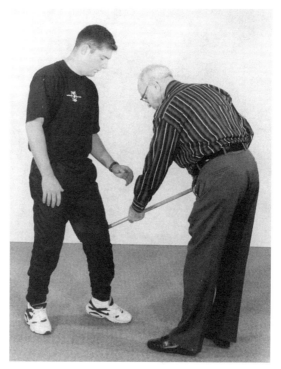

ILLUS. 9N

3 of 3

Finish with thrust to abdomen

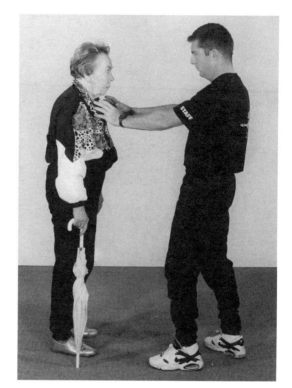

Umbrella, cane etc. can be placed behind assailant's knees

"Grounding" an assailant with a cane, umbrella, crutch, club, etc.

Tug upwards slightly and lean into assailant, causing him to fall

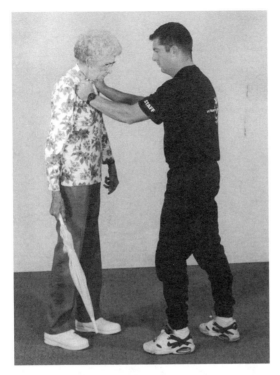

ILLUS. 9Q

1 of 3

Bring umbrella or cane over assailant's wrists/arms (radial nerve)

"Clothes grab" or "choke hold" defense with cane, umbrella, crutch, etc.

ILLUS. 9R

2 of 3

Press down hard, pinning assailant's arms and bringing him in towards you

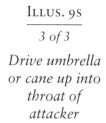

ILLUS. 9S

3 of 3

Drive umbrella or cane up into throat of attacker

CHAPTER TEN

FINAL THOUGHTS

What we have tried to present here is a "triple-layered" defense system for every potential victim of violence, whether man, woman, child, or corporate entity. This system basically consists of 1) appropriate <u>prevention and precautionary measures</u>, including a heightened awareness of potential dangers; 2) multi-faceted or flexible <u>emergency plans or policies</u> to follow through with in the event of a crisis; and 3) practical, simple, and most of all *effective* <u>self defense maneuvers</u> that will quickly and legally incapacitate an attacker.

The fact that everyone's defense system is composed of different mix-and-match components designed to custom-fit each individual and each situation, complete with alternate "back-up" techniques, is an added bonus. Since no two defense plans will be identical because the possible combinations are endless and due to the human factor, every confrontational situation is different, even if a potential attacker studies this book, he will never be able to predict or prevent whatever actions his victim might take. In fact, the suggestions made here should strike fear in the hearts of any *intelligent*, potential criminals who *do* read this book. While the Justice System may be slow or ineffective in stopping and/or punishing violent crime,[1] potential victims can, *and do*, stop criminals in their tracks every day with personal defense actions such as those suggested herein.

We are not in any way suggesting that citizens become vigilantes and single-handedly start planning to hunt down and eliminate the criminal element of society. That is, and should remain, the job of professional law enforcement officials. We do, however, encourage all individuals to maximize their capabilities and increase their safety factor without relying on outside help, which may not arrive in time, to rescue them. We challenge you to become "proactive" rather than "reactive", with a fervent determination to survive any confrontation.

We believe the information provided in this book should give you the tools to formulate your own defense plan to protect yourself and your loved ones from violent crime at home, play or at work. We must all cast aside the shadow of victimization and acquire the righteous cloak of survivorship.

Finally, in these times of diminishing knights in shining armor, *you can, and must, become your own bodyguard!*

---

[1] Roger Dale Stafford, convicted of murdering a family of three, including a 12 year old boy, who stopped to assist him with his "apparently" disabled vehicle, and of the robbery and murders of six people at the Oklahoma City Sirloin Stockade Restaurant in 1978 as mentioned in the Introduction of this book, was finally executed in July, 1995.

BIBLIOGRAPHY AND ADDITIONAL SOURCES FOR FURTHER STUDY

Kilpatrick, D.G., Edmunds, C.N., and Seymour, A. (1992). *Rape in America: A Report to the Nation.* National Victim Center, Arlington, VA 22201.

Novacek, J., Raskin, R., Bahlinger, D., Firth, L., and Rybicki, S. (1993). *Rape: Tulsa Women Speak Out.* Tulsa Institute of Behavioral Sciences, Tulsa, OK 74120.

1994 Mother's Day Report, The Older Women's League, (1994). Washington, D.C.

Bastian, L. (May, 1995). Criminal Victimization 1993. *Bureau of Justice Statistics Bulletin.* U.S. Department of Justice, 1-6.

Criminal Victimization in the United States: 1973-88 Trends, (July 1991). *Bureau of Justice Statistics, A National Crime Survey Report.* U.S. Department of Justice.

Criminal Victimization in the United States: 1973-92 Trends, (July, 1994). *Bureau of Justice Statistics, A National Crime Victimization Survey Report.* U.S. Department of Justice.

Criminal Victimization in the United States, 1990, (February 1992); 1991, (December, 1992); 1992, (March, 1994); 1993, (May, 1996) *Bureau of Justice Statistics, National Crime Victimization Survey Reports.* U. S. Department of Justice.

1993 Crime in Oklahoma, *Oklahoma State Bureau of Investigation, Uniform Crime Reports,* Robert J. Hicks, Director.

1993 Crime in Texas, The Texas Crime Report. *Texas Department of Public Safety.* Crime Records Service, Crime Information Bureau, Uniform Crime Reporting, James R. Wilson, Director.

Greenfeld, L.A. (April 1995). Prison Sentences and Time Served for Violence. *Bureau of Justice Statistics, Selected Findings.* U. S. Department of Justice, 1-3.

Zawitz, M. W., Klaus, P.A., Bachman, R., Bastian, L.D., DeBerry, Jr., M. M., Rand, M.R., and Taylor, B.M. (October, 1993). Highlights from 20 Years of Surveying Crime Victims. *Bureau of Justice Statistics,* U. S. Department of Justice.

National Update (January, 1993, Vol. II, No. 3). *Bureau of Justice Statistics,* U. S. Department of Justice.

Bachman, R. (January, 1994). Violence Against Women. *Bureau of Justice Statistics*, A National Crime Victimization Survey Report. U. S. Department of Justice, 1-14.

Violence Between Intimates (November 1994). *Bureau of Justice Statistics, Selected Findings*. U. S. Department of Justice, 1-10.

Block, R. (August, 1984). Victimization and Fear of Crime: World Perspectives. *Bureau of Justice Statistics*. U. S. Department of Justice.

Drugs, Crime, and the Justice System (December, 1992). *A National Report from the Bureau of Justice Statistics*. U. S. Department of Justice.

Harlow, C.W. (January 1991). Female Victims of Violent Crime. Bureau of Justice Statistics. U. S. Department of Justice.

Quigley, Paxton. *Armed and Female*. New York: St. Martin's Press, 1990.

Rand, M. R. (July 1990). Handgun Crime Victims. *Bureau of Justice Statistics Special Report*. U. S. Department of Justice.

The Crime of Rape (March 1985). *Bureau of Justice Statistics Bulletin*. U. S. Department of Justice.

Harlow, C. (April 1987). Robbery Victims. *Bureau of Justice Statistics Special Report*. U. S. Department of Justice.

Langan, P. A. and Cunniff, M. A. (February, 1992). Recidivism of Felons on Probation, 1986 - 89. *Bureau of Justice Statistics Special Report*. U. S. Department of Justice.

Allen-Hagen, B., Sickmund, M., and Snyder, H. N. (November, 1994). Juveniles and Violence: Juvenile Offending and Victimization. *Office of Juvenile Justice and Delinquency Prevention*. U. S. Department of Justice.

Finkelhor, D., Hotaling, G., and Sedlak, A. (May, 1990). Missing, Abducted, Runaway, and Thrownaway Children in America. *Office of Juvenile Justice and Delinquency Prevention*. U. S. Department of Justice.

Gates, Daryl F. "Chief, My Life in the LAPD". New York: Bantam Books, 1992, p. 302 - 304.

Rand, M. R. (August, 1993). Crime and the Nation's Households, 1992. *Bureau of Justice Statistics Bulletin*. U. S. Department of Justice.

Bastian, L. D. and Taylor, B. M. (September, 1991). School Crime. Bureau of Justice Statistics, *A National Crime Victimization Survey Report*. U. S. Department of Justice.

Langan, P. A. and Innes, C. A. (August 1986). Preventing Domestic Violence Against Women. *Bureau of Justice Statistics Special Report*. U. S. Department of Justice.

Fatal Workplace Injuries in 1993: A Collection of Data and Analysis. (June, 1995). *Bureau of Labor Statistics*. U. S. Department of Labor.

Toscano, G. (August 1995). News Release: *National Census of Fatal Occupational Injuries*, 1994 - USDL-95-288. Bureau of Labor Statistics. U. S. Department of Labor. 1-10.

Toscano, G. and Weber, W. (April 1995). Violence in the Workplace. *Office of Safety, Health, and Working Conditions. Bureau of Labor Statistics*. U. S. Department of Labor.

Gottfredson, M. and Hirschi, T. "A General Theory of Crime". Stanford, California: Stanford University Press, 1990.

Harvey, M. G. and Cosier, R. A. (Undated and Unpublished Report). Homicides in the Workplace, The Hidden Killer. *The College of Business Administration, University of Oklahoma*, Norman, OK 73019.

Fear and Violence in the Workplace: A Survey Documenting the Experience of American Workers. (October, 1993). *Northwestern National Life, Employee Benefits Division*. Minnesota.

NIOSH National Profile, 1993. *National Institute of Safety and Health*. Centers for Disease Control and Prevention. U. S. Department of Health and Human Services.

Toscano, G. and Windau, J. (October, 1994). The Changing Character of Fatal Work Injuries. *Monthly Labor Review, Bureau of Labor Statistics*. Department of Labor.

NIOSH Alert: Preventing Homicide in the Workplace. (September, 1993). *Centers for Disease Control and Prevention, National Institute of Safety and Health*. U. S. Department of Health and Human Services.

Fatal Injuries to Workers in the United States, 1980 - 1989; A Decade of Surveillance. (August, 1993). *National Institute for Occupational Safety and Health*. Centers for Disease Control and Prevention, U. S. Department of Health and Human Services.

Bachman, R. (October, 1992). Elderly Victims. *Bureau of Justice Statistics Special Report*. U. S. Department of Justice. 1-9.

Dunston, M. S. "Street Signs". Wisconsin: Performance Dimensions Publishing, 1992.

SOURCES FOR FURTHER TRAINING OR INFORMATION

Self Defense Training:

American Women's Self
Defense Association (AWSDA)
c/o Elizabeth Kennedy,
Executive Director
713 North Wellwood Ave.
Lindenhurst,NY. 11757
(516) 225-6262*

*Call for AWSDA
representative in your area

Defensive Concepts, Inc.
c/o James D. Daniels
10860 Paint Creek Road
Greenfield, OH 45123
(513) 981-2396

The Defensive Edge
c/o John Moore
2803 Heritage Dr.
Champaign, IL. 61821
(217) 351-7407

McClintock Self-Defense
c/o Patti McClintock
4560 Alvarado Canyon Rd.,
Suite 1F
San Diego, CA 92120
(619) 281-6500

Modern Warrior
c/o Phil Messina
711 N. Wellwood Ave.
Lindenhurst, NY. 11757
(516) 226-8383

Options for Personal Safety
c/o Andy Stafford
2009 Lakewood Drive
Sebring, FL 33872
(813) 382-0180

PAP Associates
c/o Chuck Dolan
P. O. Box 1032
Piscataway, NJ 08855-1032
(908) 777-2069

Personal Power – Assault
Prevention Training
c/o Judith Weiss
P. O. Box 684984
Austin, TX 78768
(512) 442-4256

Pro Systems
c/o Joseph Truncale
P. O. Box 261
Glenview, IL 60025
(847) 729-7681

Tidewater Academy, Home of
Rape Aggression Defense
Systems (RAD)
c/o Larry Nadeau or
Sheri Iachetta
498A Wythe Creek Road
Poquoson, VA 23662
(804) 868-4400*

*Call for RAD instructors in
your area

Thompson Relative Arts
c/o Penny Thompson
P. O. Box 691954
Tulsa, OK 74169-1954
(918) 664-5046

Ultimate Survivors, Inc.
c/o Janice Seifert, President
P. O. Box 2036
Claremore, OK 74018
(918) 584-4946

Firearms training:

The Firearms Academy
of Seattle
c/o Gila May-Hayes
P. O. Box 400
Onalaska, WA 98570
(360) 978-6102

Lethal Force Institute
c/o Masaad Ayoob
P. O. Box 122
Concord, NH 03302
1-800-624-9049

National Law Enforcement
Training Center (NLETC)
c/o Jim Lindell, President
1710 Walnut, Suite 102
Kansas City, MO 64108
1-800-782-8323
Fax (816) 474-2030

TO ORDER

What Do You Do When You Can't Call A Cop?

ISBN 0-9657443-0-2

SHIP TO

Name _____

Address _____

City/State/Zip _____

Phone _____

_____ Books @ $13.95 = _____

5.5% Oklahoma sales tax if applicable = _____

Shipping and handling @ $2.50 = _____

Each additional book @ $.50 = _____

Total = _____

Send order to: **Ultimate Survivors , Inc.**
P.O. Box 2036
Claremore, OK 74018

Please call (918) 584-4946 for shipping quotes on large orders.